OPEN YO...

with *Bicycling*

"Shawn's fervent love for cycling is obvious.
In fact, it practically rides off the pages.
He has written a thorough and practical guide
for beginners looking to take up cycling
or individuals who wish to learn more about
the cycling culture and community."

—Tiffany M. Reiss, Ph.D, Department Chair,
Exercise Science and Wellness, Bastyr University

"The book is chock-full of useful information
on a myriad of topics ranging from entering the
bicycle business to what cyclists should eat. In my
case, I found my passion for riding in my mid thirties
and wish that it would have been earlier in my life.
[This] book will help others in this regard
and I recommend it."

—Stan Gregg, President, Gregg's Cycles, Inc. (www.greggscycles.com)
"#3 bicycle shop in the U.S." –*Velo Business Magazine*

OPEN YOUR HEART
with *Bicycling*

Mastering Life through Love of the Road

SHAWN B. ROHRBACH

DreamTime Publishing, Inc.

DreamTime Publishing, Inc., books are available at special quantity discounts for bulk purchases for sales promotions, premiums, fund raising, and educational needs. Please contact us at www.DreamTimePublishing.com for additional information.

978-1-60166-003-9

Library of Congress Control Number: 2006931927

Trademarks used herein are for the benefit of the respective trademark owners.

Branding, website, and cover design for DreamTime Publishing by
    Rearden Killion • www.reardenkillion.com
Illustrations by Janice Marie Phelps • www.janicephelps.com
Manuscript consulting by Jeannette Cézanne • www.customline.com
Text layout and design by Gary A. Rosenberg • www.garyarosenberg.com

This publication is designed to provide accurate and authoritative information in regard to the subject matter covered. It is sold with the understanding that the publisher is not engaged in rendering legal, accounting, or other professional service. If legal advice or other expert assistance is required, the services of a competent professional person should be sought.

> —From a declaration of principles jointly adopted by a committee of the
> American Bar Association and a committee of publishers.

Readers should consult with a physician before undertaking any exercise, fitness, or diet program.

This book is printed on recycled, acid-free paper
containing a minimum of 50% recycled, de-inked fiber.

Contents

Note from the Publisher

Balancing the overall mission of a series of books with each author's individual creativity and vision is an enjoyable and rewarding challenge. The goal of this note is to tie the loose ends together to make your experience with this book as meaningful as possible.

We have two goals with the Open Your Heart series. One is to provide you with practical advice about your hobby or interest, in this case bicycling. We trust this advice will increase your ongoing enjoyment of the sport, or perhaps even encourage you to rediscover your love of a childhood activity.

Our second goal is to help you use what you know and love to make the rest of your life happier and easier. This process worked in different ways for each of our writers, so it will likely work in different ways for each of you. For some, it's a matter of becoming more self-aware. Just realizing what makes you happy on the road, and then gradually learning to use those feelings as a barometer when dealing with your job, relationships, and other issues could be an important first step. For others, bicycling provides an important outlet for stress and contemplation, allowing you to go back into your daily life refreshed. For yet others, you might discover how to meditate, how to connect with the mysterious flow of the Universe when you are immersed in cycling. Once you recognize the beauty of that for what it is, you can then learn to connect with the flow in other ways at other times.

We are not suggesting you will find all of your answers in this book. We are, though, inviting you to look at something you love with new eyes, a new perspective, and a new heart. Once you recognize the importance of feeling good in one area of your life, you are open to feeling good in the rest of your life. And that is the cornerstone to mastering your life.

Happy reading!

Meg Bertini

Meg Bertini
Publisher

For my mother,
for all of your great cooking
throughout the years.

Acknowledgements

Other than my parents, there have been three primary influences in my life. First, Fr. Augustine Kalberer OSB, my primary professor of philosophy, assured me it is okay to be smart. Second, Will Luden taught me to do my work well and not to take myself too seriously. Finally, Keith Abbot and Bobbie Louise Hopkins tried to teach me how to write.

Preface

Let our people travel light and free
on their bicycles.

—EDWARD ABBEY, *DESERT SOLITAIRE*

When I was approached to write a book about bicycling, I was determined not to write another repair manual or a book about how to win every race you enter. There are many useful books on the market about specific styles of cycling, including fitness, recreational, and BMX riding.

What I didn't see on the market was a book that spoke directly to *why* I ride my bike as much as I do. I've realized over the years that there are many of us who live for cycling. Why is that? It's such a simple machine, and it hurts so much riding up steep hills. I set out to explore this passion—in myself, and in others.

During the process of writing, interviewing, and editing, I discovered that everyone who rides a bike seriously has a fixation on food. No wonder! Cycling burns more calories than most other exercises. I began to ask fellow cyclists about food, and it became a standard topic of conversation every time I met a new cyclist. I incorporated that topic as a thread throughout the book. In chapter

Calories Burned

At the website, www.aquasphereusa.com/fit_calories.html, you will find a comparison of calories burned per hour by type of exercise. Weightlifting will burn 215 calories, while walking for the same amount of time will burn 325. Cycling for one hour will burn 720 calories, the same as one hour of running.

four, I talk about the importance of food and even see food as a spiritual exercise in its own right. I make a promise in that same chapter to include recipes for my favorite foods from my mother's kitchen, and they can be found in Appendix One.

The subject of road rage inevitably comes up when talking with serious cyclists. It is not a pleasant subject, but I felt it was necessary to include some thoughts on it in a book that speaks about the heart. My take on the subject—both personally and after considering the topic for this book—is that it can be minimized. I explore strategies for reducing risk of engagement in a road rage incident in order to encourage people to consider getting on a bike and riding frequently.

Finally, my hope is to treat the subject intelligently; that is, not to tell you how to do something, but rather give suggestions for how to think about it and find your own best practices, especially in areas such as choosing a style of cycling and buying a bike.

As this book is being submitted to the publisher, a group of cyclists known as Bike4peace and centered in Everett, Washington, are leaving their homes for a bicycle ride across the country to Washington, D.C., to help us think about our dependence on oil and whether there is a connection to the country's current wars. I was able to interview two members of the group via email as they busily prepared to leave. And, yes, even demonstrators for peace have favorite foods!

This book is for all cyclists, from beginners to those who are highly experienced. For those of you just now learning about cycling, there is much to learn and love about the sport. I intend to give you solid information, motivation, and a keen desire to find out why so many people love cycling. For the truly avid, we all continue to learn more, and I offer insights from activists, civic planners, racers, devoted commuters, and others who will certainly help you think about cycling in a new and positive way. For those who may want more details on some of the words, brands, etc., mentioned, I've included a glossary.

My personal experience with cycling has spanned almost forty years, and each year I enjoy it more than ever. Cycling is my primary source of regular exercise; it generates physical and emotional energy, provides time for thinking, and often offers what can only be called a metaphysical experience.

As I prepared to write this book, I realized that, for many people, cycling goes beyond being occasional recreation or a form of exercise—it becomes a part of the fabric of their lives. That is ultimately what I intend to explore here.

Shawn Rohrbach

INTRODUCTION

It's a Long Road to Nirvana

Fasten your seatbelt;
it's going to be a bumpy night
—BETTY DAVIS *ALL ABOUT EVE*

I recently rode a standard training route familiar to most serious Seattle-based cyclists. The route uses the bicycle lane on the I-90 floating bridge across Lake Washington; the designated bicycle path continues across Mercer Island to Bellevue. The route, however, veers off this path and follows the main street that circumnavigates Mercer Island.

The main point of interest on this ride is the very technical turn on the east side of the island. The route is popular among cyclists, but definitely not among local residents, as hundreds of cyclists descend on the small island every weekend!

One steep hill in particular separates the serious from the merely curious. This route offers some very technical cycling: steep descents and extremely tight cornering both up- and down-hill. The route is mostly covered with large deciduous trees and in the middle of a hot summer offers abundant shade. The local residents are usually very patient and are careful to allow cyclists their legal space on the road. The ride is exhilarating and easily accessible from Seattle.

One cyclist tagged along with our group and drafted behind us for several miles. Drafting allows a cyclist to travel long distances with relatively little effort. A good cyclist will ask a group for permission to draft, but this particular cyclist did not. I sprinted a short, steep hill toward the end, leaving the cyclist well behind us for the remainder of the ride. As we sat in the small park adjacent to the commuting trail and waited for him to catch up, it struck me then that it had been almost thirty-five years to the day since I had first ridden on the very same route when I was fifteen. The only difference was that the I-90 freeway had not yet been built and access around Mercer Island was by way of an old bridge with a narrow and dangerous sidewalk.

Over these thirty-five years, I've slowly become the person I wanted to be. I arrived here by embarking on and nurturing an intentional spiritual journey, and a simple bicycle has always been an integral part of the journey. I began to reflect on that and the result is this book.

There is always a first bike. Mine was a Columbia single speed. It was freedom! I no longer walked to the store: I rode. I received it for Christmas when I was thirteen, and in spite of a rare snowfall, I insisted on riding anyway. The Seattle area will typically get only a few inches each winter, but that year we enjoyed a two-foot slam at Christmas.

I rode that Columbia until it rusted out and was barely functional.

This affair I have with cycling really began, though, when I was fifteen. My parents decided to take the family to Europe. Before that trip, I had only an inkling of how seriously the rest of the world takes cycling. During the summer of 1971, while traveling with my family in Vienna, Austria, I bought a Puch Bergmeister. The salesman, in fairly good English, told me the very same bike had been in the Tour de France the year before. I think he knew a sucker when he saw one. He said the person riding it did not win, but when we walked out of the shop I didn't care. At fifteen, I had a real bike.

It is significant that I fantasized the Puch having been in the Tour de France. Just as there is always a first bike, there are also dreams that never come true . . . like riding in the Tour de France. Not necessarily winning, just being able to ride. I never actually got there—despite having bought, in Europe, a tour-level bicycle.

But that's how my real spiritual journey begins: with a world-class bicycle, a dream, and the haunting realization that no matter what the hucksters on television say, not every dream comes true. You can't have it all, but you *can* have what you truly desire. I needed to learn this lesson, and I discovered the simpler pursuits like cycling gave me exactly what I desired. Not achieving boyhood dreams has been the least of my worries, and the joy that I experience on a daily basis began when I understood that as a young adult.

I have had intense exposure to the spiritual practices of two major religious disciplines, Roman Catholicism and Buddhism. Both are known for meaningful and deeply rooted traditions of ritualized spiritual practices, with a reason or significance for almost every word and movement. These spiritual practices intend to assist the individual practitioner in achieving a grace-filled life or in enjoying enlightenment.

While these practices have helped millions of people achieve their spiritual goals, they did nothing for me. They were interesting to observe, and I appreciated that they were important to people like my mother and my writing professors, but they didn't work for me. Nor did any other organized religious system.

A spiritual practice, however, is essential. The lazy, slothful, or intentionally evil rarely achieve grace and enlightenment. While I have been all three at some point in my fifty years, I am more disciplined and good than lazy and evil. And I did find a practice that facilitated the great internal growth I have enjoyed. People come to terms with this at various ages, typically later in life. Some never do. I came to this reality early, not through my Church, but through my reading and spending numerous hours studying rocks and birds. My own kind of spirituality solidified when I was thirteen as I sat under the dining room table watching Neil Armstrong walk on the moon. I comprehended then the magnitude of creation and the complexity of life. It was more then hymns and communion. I wanted that understanding to be a part of my metaphysical discovery, and it will always remain a part of it.

The psychiatrist Viktor Frankl wrote several books with consistent themes, one of which was that you not only have the opportunity to live a good or a great life, but you have the *responsibility* to do so. I believe this and have always known that a disciplined practice would reward me in far greater ways that a cheap and easy methodology. I never found satisfaction in simple acquisitions of toys or in mindless television, and I have never experienced immediate religious conversion.

I first became mildly aware that cycling was more than transportation or exercise for me during the winter of 1972 as I commuted on my bicycle to high school. I was training for an extended tour of the Seattle, Vancouver, and Victoria triangle. I began to train in Feb-

Falls Hill is an unofficial name for the road that leads from Fall City to Snoqualmie, Washington. At the top of the hill is the view point where visitors can view the magnificent Snoqualmie Falls.

ruary, and as my legs grew stronger I rode the Falls Hill more frequently and it became consequently easier. Besides experiencing increased fitness, however, I also experienced something I had never expected.

I discovered on these commuting rides that I was processing

schoolwork in my head. Once I got to the classroom, the information I had read the night before was well grounded in my mind and available for me to use in discussion and lab work. I could "write" a paper in my head as I rode. At school, I would sit at the typewriter and in minutes flesh out a reasonably good first draft that often served as the final product. Subsequently, my grades improved, and as I finished my junior year, I was a four-point-average student. And a physically strong one.

I was certainly not fully aware then of what cycling would ultimately become for me and the power this practice would have in continually renewing my energy and internal growth, ultimately giving me the gift that is the life I enjoy now. Something kept me at it. Maybe it was my adolescent fantasy of riding in the Tour de France. Not that it matters. I kept at it, and that's all that counts.

Some might dismiss cycling as an amusing recreation or a simple method for attaining a consistent level of fitness. For me it was one of the most important factors in becoming a whole and complete human being.

> Eastern Washington is a distinct region. Washington is almost evenly divided by the Cascade Mountains. To the west, where rain is abundant, the region is green and fertile while to the east, where rain is blocked by the mountains, the region is dry.

My senior year of high school ended with our family moving and beginning the construction of our hotel in Eastern Washington. Between making preparations to enter college, working full time in my father's construction company, and building the hotel, I had no time for cycling that summer. For the first time, I began to recognize just how important cycling was for me.

This became evident as I embarked on my college education in a Catholic seminary. I didn't know it then, but this would become the most important disruption in my spiritual journey.

As I prepared to enter the seminary, I thought the journey as I saw it then would continue and in fact progress. A well-established monastic community offered so much promise for my spiritual journey, and certainly much promise exists there for those so inclined. My personality had become intelligently independent to the point my father was constantly nervous about the books I was reading—like St. Augustine's *City of God*. This is a book typically reserved for students of theology; Augustine attempts to put the creation story of seven days into a realistic context. Most adherents to literal interpretation of Scripture dismiss this book. I, however, understood what Augustine wanted to say: the creation story is a myth in the true sense of the word.

I moved into my dormitory, leaving my Puch Bergmeister behind at home. That first year I suffered ear infections, the flu, toothaches, corns on my feet, lower-back dislocation, loneliness, and a hatred for the sequence of events that put me in that place. Psychologists would enjoy analyzing the earliest of these events, but the overriding influence causing this outcome finds its source in a desire to please. While it is perhaps a good thing to please, this desire cannot be the motivation behind any decision that shapes a person's life.

I remember having made a decision in the past that hadn't pleased my father; I was adamant that I was going to ride my bike to Vancouver, B.C. I made the trip in spite of his strident objections. But by the time I was eighteen, I had already forgotten the value of this decision.

I was told to look on this time as a rebuilding, shedding the old me and putting on the new me, something like what I might find in the letters of St. Paul. I tried to see it that way, and I failed. I made it through to spring, passed my finals, and arrived back home ready to work another summer. I pulled my Puch Bergmeister from the barn and rode up the Icicle Creek valley and skinny-dipped in the snow-cold river.

I was free again.

I rode every day I could between working construction and tending to the gardens around the hotel. I was free again, able to process thoughts and actually make some sense of the previous ten months in that damp, dark seminary.

It is amazing what happens when you get back on the saddle, spend hours tapping out the miles and doing nothing but thinking. I learned then to trust the thinking I did as my legs rose up and down, at a consistent cadence, mile after mile. I dried out, tanned, and by the end of the summer was back in physical, mental, and spiritual form.

During the summer I also looked around for another school. The cost of the seminary then was fifteen hundred dollars for the year, which included tuition and room and board. I would never get through the University of Washington for that amount. There was no family money for school, and I knew I didn't want to be a carpenter for the rest of my life. The rector of the seminary liked me and invited me back in spite of my declaration that I had no intention of becoming a priest. Our conversations focused on my potential, that it would be good if I kept my options open. I said I would, but it was more important for me to get what value I could from this education. It was agreed I could come back. I decided to take the Puch and my skis, along with my ropes, crampons, and harnesses with me.

The farmland surrounding the seminary was punctuated with short, steep hills, and there was little traffic. I usually rode in the morning, as most of my classes were in the afternoon. I would take off on Saturday after chores and ride, sometimes reaching Vancouver and making it back in time for vespers, a sixty-mile round trip. I also brought my skis and mountaineering equipment. All in all, I spent more time outside than I did studying, yet still achieving a respectable three-point-four grade point average.

I thrived that year.

In the spring, I discovered an early racing season in the Lower Mainland, a geographical location that the media picked up as a formal name, and entered, even though I was not properly dressed or equipped. I rode mostly road races, averaging twenty to sixty miles. I finished most and actually placed third in one.

Without the Puch and my Fischer skis, I would have dropped out and would probably have never gone back to school. In any case, I decided not to return to the seminary for my third year. I took a year off to sort out a suspicious desire to enter a Jesuit novitiate in Portland, Oregon. I entered on August 15, 1976, and lasted until November first of that year. Again, no bicycle, and my life was completely miserable. I went home and worked construction, skied, and rode the Puch. An idyllic life without direction. I decided to return to the seminary and complete my bachelor's degree.

The monks allowed me to return without stipulations. I was predictable; they knew and understood me. My third year began with formal coursework in metaphysics, and I enjoyed this. Between my cycling, mountaineering, skiing, and reading, I had found an intellectual and spiritual home. While others struggled with Duns Scotus and Kant, I got it.

Philosophy is best when actively lived rather than passively contemplated. This came out clearly in my papers, and my professor, Father Augustine Kalberer, with his infinite patience, recognized my grasp and tolerated my excessive outdoor activities. He saw the results clearly while more studious classmates clucked and sniped about my lack of library time. It was nice to get on the bike and roll away from the seminary alone and in silence, away from the gossip, wagging tongues, and excessive value judgments.

As I entered the seminary for my last year, the rector knew I was going to finish my studies at the end of the year, but he approved my enrollment anyway. He wanted me to complete my education, and the seminary was then not an accredited institution; my credits might not transfer to a U.S.-based university. It was a repeat of the previous year without apologies. I bicycled, climbed, skied, studied a bit and succeeded in failing only one course. I got what I wanted from my professors and thanked them. In many ways they made my good life a reality. I packed my equipment and accumulated books and moved home with the intent of finding work or studies somewhere else. I had grown more and more independent and was not turning back.

During that time I was fortunate enough to be enrolled in a geology courses taught by Father Nichola Ruh, and in it I found a subject I truly loved. To this day, as I ride, I study the terrain and try to understand how each hill I climb or river I cross was formed. Combined with my rock climbing skills, this new passion had me searching for graduate schools where I could transfer my philosophy degree into a master's in geology, but no such possibility existed.

I was totally broke and therefore I took a job driving a taxi in Lynnwood, Washington. We were embarking on one of the worst recessions the country had known outside of the great Depression, and there was no need for someone with a degree in medieval philosophy. My spiritual journey was abruptly and painfully interrupted once again.

The word "journey" perhaps implies going somewhere. Various wise people differ on whether the actual journey is more important, or if the end game should be the primary focus. Since I have already admitted that I don't know where my spiritual journey will take me, I cannot place much importance yet on the end. I would also be rather sad if after the struggle that has been so much a part of this journey, it never ends and the only important thing will be the quality of the next step. I think I need an ending, some sort of closure.

Like cycling, the journey encounters steep hills and easy flats.

People cut me off and help me along; I can go for months without flat tires and then have three in the same day. That's as far as I want to take that obvious comparison. I want to focus on what might be considered progress or insight. I have managed to learn, and in learning have managed to become better at some things. This has in turn resulted in my becoming a better person.

That's the most obvious spiritual benefit: cycling is a repetitious motion, and it is precisely this repetition that begins to bring these fractured elements together. The pedaling and breathing are key. As a seminarian, I learned the value of meditation from the Benedictine monks. One spiritual director taught me to select four or five different locations and postures, emphasizing the value of rhythmic breathing and the need to spend this time undisturbed. It dawned on me fairly soon I already knew this from cycling.

As for the rest of the interruptions along this journey, I can only say they are mostly self-inflicted. I admire people who can genuinely stay on track. I loathe people who pretend to. I was told once I deserve myself, and that is absolutely correct. For the most part I am a good person with the best of intentions. I have learned to keep my eyes on the road. As a result I don't hit the glass and nails as often and get so many flats.

As a young man, these events could have been interpreted as catastrophic. Age allows for a different, calmer perspective. My journey was off to a rough start, but so what? Certainly I could have given up and become an emotional and financial burden on some hapless sucker who would give me endless consolation and money. I know people who do this. I am one of these crazy people who actually like the steep hills. There have been numerous interruptions in this journey and considering I probably have about thirty-five years to go until I die, I anticipate there will be more.

What I'm going to do here is examine how riding a bicycle became my spiritual practice. I am assured by my Catholic and

Buddhist friends that this really isn't a serious spiritual practice. They insist I need to kneel in church and count rosary beads or let some meditation master whip me with a stick for it to be a real and valuable practice. I disagree. I'll let you be the judge. My time spent at Naropa University, a Buddhist college in Boulder, Colorado, reaffirmed my discovery: that cycling, more than any religion, has provided me with the challenges, insights and rewards to truly understand who I am in the eyes of God.

I am most true to myself when riding.

ONE

Different Styles, Same Results

Let me tell you what I think of bicycling. I think it has done more to emancipate women than anything else in the world. It gives women a feeling of freedom and self-reliance. I stand and rejoice every time I see a woman ride by on a wheel . . . the picture of free, untrammeled womanhood.

—Susan B. Anthony

One of the great controversies in the lives of many Catholics comes as a result of reexamining the rituals of the mass, especially in what is physically expected of participants during the Eucharistic prayer. Many traditionalist Catholics believe it is necessary to kneel during this prayer to show appropriate devotion and reverence. Others feel it is perfectly acceptable to stand as the new rituals allow. I do not enter into the fray on this or usually on any other religious dispute, but both sides of this debate stress the need to show reverence and devotion.

I was required to take a class on meditation when I attended Naropa University, a small college in Boulder, Colorado, with a Buddhist tradition. I am athletic, but not very flexible in my joints. As I attempted to sit cross-legged on my pillow, the person teaching the meditation practice scowled at me. I gave up attempting to achieve the lotus position and sat against the wall with my legs flat out. The scowling persisted until I finally just left the room, to the great delight, I am sure, of the stricter practitioners.

The debates between various religious faiths can cause war. The hatred felt by some who profess to be Muslim for Jews is notorious. Not only are they debating the practice of certain rituals, some of the most extreme seek to kill each other. This exists in any faith. My own Catholic upbringing was fraught with debate over whether to blame Jews for the death of Jesus on one hand, and on the other verbal assaults from Evangelical protestants asserting that I was going straight to hell because I was a Catholic.

The same type of rigidity exists in cycling and does more than anything else to deter people from taking up the exercise or from participating in the sport. I find a great similarity between the harsh and narrow-minded religious leaders of my past and many of the cyclists with whom I no longer choose to ride. In fact, the cyclists are often much worse! Cycling is, for them, a cult experience. The list of requirements for acceptance can be longer than the list of qualifications to become a Catholic. It can be extremely exclusive. Everything from the bike itself to the type of sock worn fall within narrow parameters, and anyone outside of the acceptable range falls victim to wrathful scorn.

A former Olympic cyclist told me a story about becoming so upset with the rigid approach to training and competition that he once entered a track race at the master's level on a three-speed Raleigh and won a pursuit race. The purists wanted him banned from future races, but only the time commitment to his family and business kept him from returning. He still threatens to return now—at age seventy.

What he was showing, of course, is how silly it is to adhere to norms that mean absolutely nothing intrinsically. These racers use expensive bikes devoted only to track racing, and they didn't want an old man beating them on an antique three-speed that anyone could afford; it took away their cachet, their claims to exclusivity.

I ride over Snoqualmie Pass in Washington State at least three times a year. Last summer I was riding with a young man training for a small independent club in Seattle. He laughed at an elderly man riding what is known as a "comfy" bike: a modified mountain bike that has been outfitted with large, easy-to-reach handlebars and a fat, soft seat. We passed the man along the first rise above Edgewick Road. As we powered up in the July heat, we stopped only to repair two flats. The last flat happened less than a quarter mile from the summit and, just as we were filling the tire, the man passed us and beat us to the top.

So what can we learn from that? It's true that any sport demands safety rules. A cyclist should wear a helmet and keep to the right unless passing. A cyclist should not ride too closely to another to be drafted unless they both agree to the arrangement. But beyond the safety precautions, nothing is left—except personal preferences.

I normally ride a Torrelli road bicycle with a steel frame and Campagnolo components. I also ride a Bianchi track bike with fixed gear that doesn't allow coasting or back-pedaling. I am fitting an old Ochsner bicycle with gear appropriate for cyclo-cross racing with the ambition of trying to compete in that once again in the near future. I presently do not own a mountain bike, but will acquire one again soon. I keep looking under the Christmas tree for a Redline BMX , but that hasn't happened yet. Maybe if I am good this year. . . .

I used to commute to work every day for more than eight years, my work clothes neatly folded in my backpack. As I climbed the hill going home, cyclists in spandex would pass me, making mean-spirited comments. I didn't dress for what might be considered race training; I dressed for the Seattle weather and that usually included rain jackets, thick pants, and gloves. I commented on this to someone I saw every day also commuting, and he was derisive about what he referred to as the "wannabe racers." He wore baggy shorts and made a crude comment about men in spandex. He was no more understanding of them than they were of him. It is not surprising to find some intolerance among devoted cyclists. The important thing to remember is this is supposed to be enjoyable, so dress comfortably.

Many people pass the point in their lives where they feel the need to identify and ridicule the perceived shortcomings of others. They move on and simply accept the reality of the human experience. Others, unfortunately, do not, and dwell on their own perceived superiority. I'm certain this characteristic is evident in other pursuits, but I am most acutely aware of it in cycling. It's another lesson learned: I'll never rid the world of war, pestilence, or snide remarks. My hope is that you find a style of cycling, enjoy it, and use it to your enrichment.

Ready? Then let's go buy a bike that fits both your style and your body. The first step is not to look at *bikes,* but to shop for a shop.

I visited the town of Chimayo in New Mexico. Legend has it that when a believer kisses the dirt inside the old church, miracles can happen. I've also visited the shrine of Fatima in southern France, where it is also held that when a believer drinks or washes with the water there, miracles can happen.

Notwithstanding the miracles—which may certainly have happened—I was put off by the number of street vendors and hawkers at both sites selling religious artifacts, water samples, and small containers of dirt.

I doubt anyone really believes that possessing a statue of Jesus or Buddha brings them closer to anything. These artifacts are much like the small rocks I collected when I traveled. I love the study of geology and when I travel, I read about the local geological formations and try to collect rocks that are representative of these formations. These are mementos. I recall the trip just by feeling the rocks.

So it's hardly surprising that I look for shops so devoted to cycling that they are willing to stock not only the best bicycles on the market, but a healthy supply of bicycle kitsch—key chains with a bicycle motif, Christmas tree ornaments in the shape of antique bicycles, drink coasters with bicycle team and manufacturer logos, children's cycling kits with big name team colors and logos, coffee mugs with team logos, tiepins with a bicycle wheel, all that sort of thing. This tells me they live, eat, and breathe bicycles.

I enjoy visiting bicycle shops in other cities, especially in a foreign city. I know the big shops in Milan, Italy, fairly well. The shops in mountainous regions are more interesting, often family businesses located in someone's basement. I usually spot the racing pictures somewhere over the cash register; they are always a slimmer, more handsome version of the shop owner. I used to buy water bottles if they carried the insignia of the shop or the local town, but they've become scarce (people usually want brand name *everything,* and the local imprints are hard to find now). These are

If you are buying your first bike, I recommend you ask the bike sales person:

- What style of riding is this bike for?
- What bike do you ride?
- Do you tune the gears and brakes when you assemble the bikes?
- How high should my seat be?
- Do I get a free thirty-day safety check or tune up?
- Do you ride every bike you assemble before selling it?

the kinds of shops I really trust. These people sell a love of cycling, not just bicycles.

I visit shops when I travel because they give me real insights into local customs and culture. When I traveled to Europe with my family, we also started visiting ski shops, and even now, as "mature" adults, we cannot pass up a shop we've never been in.

When I visit a shop, I pick up the front end of the new bikes and twist the handle bar back and forth. I usually feel a headset that's too tight and will therefore grind the bearings down fast, requiring a major overhaul. This is caused by mechanics who don't know how to adjust a headset properly. They pull the bike out of the box, have fifteen minutes to assemble it, tighten down the headset so it won't come off in a test ride, and call it good to go. The bike is never properly adjusted.

To understand how to buy a bicycle, visit a shop where the owner tries to talk you *out* of buying one. This might sound absurd, but it might be precisely because they do not have one for you. I worked in a shop owned by Fred and Ruth Karacas in Port Orchard, Washington. They are truly devout Christians who live their lives according to their firmly held beliefs. I think their second religion, however, is cycling. The shop is a menagerie of Fred's racing bikes, some new bikes for sale, and a thousand bikes lining every square inch of floor space, bikes in the process of being renovated or repaired. I wanted to work in a shop and Fred wanted to fly airplanes to fight forest fires that summer. I had turned forty, was fed up with the dot-com race for instant wealth and wanted a dramatic change of pace. He tested my wrench skills and knew I could sell, and I was hired.

I know a few priests who really love celebrating the mass and look forward to every moment they spend doing this. I found the same excitement and passion in opening the shop and making the first sale of the day. Usually this was a parts sale or a repair job, something to keep the bike on the road, but it didn't matter: the interaction was everything.

We repaired the inexpensive bikes you find at discount super-stores. They're cheaply made and therefore affordable to many low- or moderate-income families. They break easily, though, and many shops won't repair them; they actually have signs stating they won't touch certain brands of bikes. That feels like the day I was refused entrance into a Catholic church for mass. I was wearing blue jeans and was told by the usher they didn't allow scum on the premises. I will gladly repair any bike, any time.

Every shop I go into has its shop rats: adolescent boys who just hang out in bike shops. I gauge the quality of the shop by the number and quality of the shop rats. They aren't wayward youths; they're aspiring racers or shop owners, fascinated with the bike culture. They often serve as the eyes and ears of the busy shop owner, thwarting theft and showing customers where things are.

I was a church rat throughout my teen years, donning a surplice and cassock and holding large candles as I helped the priest. At least the shops rats got a discount on their bike equipment for hanging around and catching thieves!

There are many unscrupulous shop owners who will sell any bike on the floor, regardless of the type of cycling the individual wants to pursue. Buy a bike that doesn't fit, ride it, and have fun—right? To my mind, this is as serious a moral issue as the old selling of indulgences in the Church—perhaps worse. A purchased indulgence is printed on a piece of paper, and hopefully God will make good on the deal. A poorly fitted bike, or a bike used for the wrong style of cycling, can cause physical harm.

A certain shop owner was known for her ability to clear out her bikes. We would watch the proud new owners glide by on bikes too big, too small, or inappropriate for the terrain and wrongly equipped. Her shop was in a perfect location near two military bases. Traditionally transient residents who serve and move on, her customer base was always large and rarely stayed long enough to give her the bad reputation she deserved.

She didn't know me, and I decided to test how she sold her bikes. I went into the shop and started looking at low-end mountain bikes.

She jumped out from behind the cash register and told me none of those would fit me. She pointed out her racing models; even though I knew the frames were exactly the same size, she talked endlessly about how the spring-loaded frames made them a much better fit. She added that a good-looking guy like me would just not be happy on one of those cheap bikes. I noted to her the only differences between the first bike I looked at and the one she was selling me were the springs and the price, and that otherwise it was exactly the same. She laughed and said I should trust someone who had been in the bike business a long time to pick out the right bike.

I hear that same line in many bicycle shops. And used car lots.

I shop at large, national retail chains for many types of goods. I am not too proud to get a deal on soap or bicycle tubes. I also shop at independently owned stores, as I see them as a crucial part of any local economy and culture. Over beer, a business student was blaming Sam Walton, founder of Wal-Mart, for predatory marketing practices that ruined the local economy. I listened and completely disagreed. A family can go to Wal-Mart and actually afford bicycles for everyone. If someone needs a four-thousand-dollar titanium bike, they won't find it at Wal-Mart. They can spend their four thousand dollars at an independent shop. But I had to correct him; Sam Walton was a latecomer to the concept of national and even international branding of a retail environment.

When I go into a Catholic church, no matter where it is, I will find a bare altar, a crucifix, a red lantern above the Blessed Sacrament in some sort of tabernacle, some statues, fixtures on the wall representing the Way of the Cross, and pews (some padded, most not). The interior of a Catholic church has not changed much over the centuries. There are reasons these items are there and are used to support the community's liturgy.

I have only been to a few synagogues and mosques, but I find them all to be extremely similar in architecture and appointments. Sam Walton understood, as did so many retailers before him, that the concept of creating a similar environment in every location encouraged people to come. Familiarity makes people comfortable.

To serve a clientele wanting a higher grade of bicycle, shop owners are aware that these customers are attracted to a shop appointed to their level of taste. It was recently reported by a financial news network that a growing demand exists for high-end custom bicycles; people are willing to pay as much as twenty-five thousand dollars for one. The segment showed an insurance adjuster in the tony shop, asking how a bicycle could be worth twenty-five thousand dollars. The dealer calmly explained several things about the brand: the quality of the custom frame, the quality of the components, the custom paint job, and the handmade custom saddle formed to fit the client perfectly. Instead of paying a thousand dollars for a bike off the rack, the client was willing to pay twenty-five thousand dollars to have the perfect ride. The shop owner made sure everyone knew climbing hills with it still hurt, though!

If you want easy Sunday cycling, ask about "comfy" bikes, often referred to as cross-bikes or hybrids. They are a combination of mountain and road bike, and typically the handlebars are situated so the cyclist can sit up straighter. Occasional and older cyclists find this position easier on the lower back.

Many vacationers like to bump around cross-country ski trails in the summer; they should look at the wide range of mountain bikes. There is a mountain bike for all wallets, starting at very inexpensive models and rising up to the three- and four-thousand dollar range. Start simple and buy up when the terrain becomes too easy or the greater challenges are more inviting.

Racing down single-track trails and crashing over logs and rocks requires a very good full-suspension mountain bike built for that purpose.

BMX bikes offer a thrill like no other, whether the cyclist is jumping off docks into a lake or competing. These short, single-speed bikes are made for a specific type of competition and are fashion statements as well.

Touring and commuting can be accomplished on any basic bicycle and the cyclist just has to make a decision about how comfortable he or she chooses to be. There are bicycles made specifically for the grind of daily commuting and long-distance touring. The wheels tend to be sturdier and the rubber is thicker than racing-style bikes, but they endure through rough roads very well. People often confuse bikes specifically designed for cyclo-cross racing with commuter bikes, and shops will often sell cyclo-cross bicycles for this purpose. They work well for commuting and touring because cyclo-cross can be a rough sport, and the bicycles are built to take it.

If you dream of sweating through the Tour de France, get a road bike. Several types of bikes are available for each type of riding or racing that is of interest. A general all-around road bike will allow the cyclist to stretch out a bit, creating a lower profile. The cyclist should be able to easily straddle the frame, but the frame should be large enough to carry the cyclist properly over bumps and around corners. If the frame is too short, the cyclist will not enjoy the open road; the bike will feel unmanageable and jumpy underneath the rider when he or she accelerates or descends hills. If the frame is too large, the cyclist will not be able to maneuver corners well and may lose control on a freewheeling downhill.

Typically, for open road cycling where the cyclist sits on the seat and leans on the handlebars, she or he should be able to look down and see just behind the front axle. If the shop offers a custom measurement for frame fit, take advantage of the service.

There are formulas used for fitting cyclists, and the opinions as to which formula is best vary as much as the weather. Rather than dwell on these formulas, I think it best to give you the mental framework that will help formulate the proper questions when you are ready to buy a bike.

I think the same advice would be equally useful for anyone desiring to explore faith communities (churches, mosques, temples and other places of worship) that preach various interpretations of the community's holy books.

First, most cyclists are told they need a bike that is comfortable. What is the meaning of "comfort" when you are gasping for breath up a long steep hill? Is this the same definition used when hauling a trailer with a child, or careening down a steep mountain pass in a two-hundred-kilometer race? Comfort is a relative term. Perhaps the word "effective" might be a better one to describe how to fit a bicycle properly.

To race properly on an oval track, specific geometries allow for the type of head- down, power-driving and quick maneuvering that's characteristic of this type of cycling. While I told the story of the elderly gentleman who rode his Raleigh three-speed on the track and won, it probably was *not* the most effective bicycle to use!

A wide variety of bicycles can be used to effectively tow a child in a trailer. Someone might be perfectly happy with a large comfy bike that has a smaller frame. The handlebars allow the cyclist to sit more upright and the smaller frame allows for easier turning and stopping. The focus probably is not so much on speed and quick maneuvering, but on safety.

Using a bicycle for general fitness perhaps suggests the cyclist intends to take longer and increasingly more difficult rides, facing up to the challenge of distance and steep hills. My own preference is a larger frame that allows my long legs to extend almost completely on the down stroke and my upper body to stretch out. I have no problem riding fifty to one hundred miles in this posture. I don't make quick, hard turns, so I do not need as much maneuverability.

A friend who races has a variety of bicycles. One of them is designed specifically for tight, quick turning. When he races crits, he is not going to use the same geometry I use when I do long, flat rides. He wants a geometry that gets into the corner and out with relative ease. The faster and tighter he can corner, the better.

Mountain bikes are sold primarily for casual weekend use. Most shop owners know this and the fit is easy; it's not difficult to sell something the customer will enjoy for rides that are five to ten miles in length. This usually means shorter frame sets that allow more upright positioning. This is usually the bread and butter of any bike shop.

Competitive mountain biking requires a more custom fit; again, the sizing depends on the style of racing. When I tried single-track downhill racing, I preferred a very short frame. I had an extra long seat post that allowed my legs to extend when riding the flats or hills, but when it came time for the fast downhill, I wanted control of the bike. I could drop the seat down to the point I could hold it between my knees and easily control the rear wheel. Other downhill racers prefer different geometries.

Rather than accepting one of the many mathematical formulas found in shops and books, decide first what the bike will be used for. This might mean owning more than one bike.

Finally, do a little research on the proper level of components necessary for specific types of cycling. I know wealthy people who will buy the best components and never use them, simply because they can. No value judgments here, unless it's of a shop owner who tries to oversell just to make a buck.

There are variations on the classic bicycle on the market, specifically recumbent and auto-shifting bikes that are intended to make cycling more comfortable. Recumbent owners claim this type of bike eases the typical back strain one might feel riding the classic-style racing bike. Owners of the auto-shifting bikes are not concerned about which gear they are in, since it's decided for them. They just pedal along and enjoy the scenery. While many fellow cyclists scoff at the idea, my sister enjoys her auto-shifting bicycle very much and rides more than she would without it. I met up with a group of cyclists in their sixties, all riding recumbent frames. They had previously had to give up cycling because of the strain on their backs caused by conventional bikes. They could easily ride seventy or eighty miles a day sitting back in a more natural position on the recumbent.

Getting the right bicycle is not accomplished through mathematical formulas or computer software alone. The right bike will be there when the cyclist decides what to do with it.

TWO

Ride Safely

Get a bicycle. You will not regret it if you live.

—MARK TWAIN, *TAMING THE BICYCLE*

I f you are new to cycling, the more you consider personal safety and pay attention to how motorists see cyclists, the better your experience will be. A driver is legally responsible for the safe condition and operation of a motorized vehicle. A cyclist has similar responsibilities, and for the citizens of Seattle and most other cities, these are clearly spelled out in the traffic code. What is clear in this code is that cyclists are allowed to use the city's streets. Also clear are the responsibilities of both motorists and cyclists.

The Seattle.gov website posts selected provisions of the Seattle Traffic Code. These provisions are the most pertinent as they relate to the motorist/cyclist/pedestrian relationships.

During the writing of this book, I witnessed an accident in which a female triathlete was legally within her rights on a busy street. She was riding at a speed within compliance with the traffic code. She was progressing toward an intersection with a green light allowing her to pass through. An older pickup truck rumbled up behind her and took a right turn. The triathlete did not have a chance to stop and was hit by the truck on its passenger side and carried several feet until she was thrown to the ground by the force. The truck paused, then drove away. The triathlete suffered a broken leg.

Urban planners have long considered the tenuous relationship between motorized vehicles and the bicycle. Many planners believe the known lack of certain skills mandates that all cyclists must use bicycle paths. They cite the inexperience of children and occasional cyclists who often weave uncontrollably as they become familiar with the stability required to safely operate a bicycle. They also cite the noise and chaos an inexperienced cyclist can experience riding in traffic for the first time. They believe allowing cyclists to use the city streets results in more motorized vehicle and bicycle-related accidents.

Opponents of this view claim bicycle paths reduce the need to develop effective skills and results in even more accidents when the bicycle path ends and the cyclist is required to complete the ride on busy streets.

Regardless of which argument is more accurate, many people simply do not want bicycles on the streets and roads.

My occasional commute to honor a consulting contract found me cycling from Kingston, Washington, along the back roads of Kitsap County to Bainbridge Island, where I caught the ferry to Seattle. It's unfortunate that I no longer make this commute: the ride is beautiful. In relative terms, the ride was an easy one along normally unused back roads. One segment of the trip took me through the town of Squammish and on to the main highway leading into the town of Bainbridge. It was here the most honking and attempted hits took place.

Believe it or not, I do mean *attempted* hits. Often trucks and cars would swerve from the oncoming lane at me as I road along the three-foot shoulder. Or I'd hear acceleration from behind and the vehicle would pass within an inch of me. If I hadn't been a strong cyclist, the noise and wind would have sent me off the road.

Another pernicious act inflicted in Kitsap County was usually executed by drinking teenagers. As I rode, they would drive by and drop an empty beer bottle just a few feet in front of me. The bottle would shatter as I grabbed for my brakes, and it usually meant a severely damaged tire and a walk home. How would anyone feel after such a horrifying act? First there is fear—is this all they will do? Then there's the feeling of anger, augmented by a desire to get even. Finally there is the overwhelming feeling of defiance. *I will do this again and again, and they will not defeat me.*

There is an urban legend I cannot verify that has a member of the state house of representatives from Kitsap County suggesting that the only solution to the bicycle "problem" would be wider bumpers. The immediate and negative reaction accused this representative of promoting murder, but she denied having spoken the words.

If the words were not spoken, the attitude prevails, not only in Kitsap County but in many municipalities in this country. The first step toward resolving the issue is legislation—and then education.

The Traffic Code states that every person operating a bicycle on a roadway is granted the same rights and is held to the same duties as anyone operating a motorized vehicle, and the only exceptions are those where the regulations simply could not apply to a bicycle.

The statute also states the obvious: don't open your car door until you are certain there are no other motorized vehicles or bicycles that could hit your door as they pass.

Both cyclists and motorists have the same responsibility to exercise due care not to hit or obstruct pedestrians. (I'd have thought this would be obvious enough not to require a law!) Both cyclists and motorists will drive at or below the posted speed using prudence to guide their decisions.

On the other hand, while I can point to regular abuses by motorists, I can also point to regular abuses by cyclists who weave through traffic at high speeds, zip along the road until they meet traffic and then jump to the sidewalk and back to the streets and through the green light. The city of New York once debated whether it was a good idea to confiscate bicycles from cyclists who practiced this and were caught.

All motorists accept that any vehicle passing must do so on the left and will pass at a safe distance from the slower-moving vehicle, and not move again to the right until there is a safe distance between them. This applies to bicycles as well. In short, a car must move away from the cyclist and not try to force the bicycle off the street. This code section would also govern the actions stated previously, where cyclists weave through traffic, causing motorists to jam on their brakes.

Contrary to what some would want, a bicycle can be ridden as close to the right side of the roadway as is safe, even if that means within the white line; the motorized vehicle must be aware of its presence and pass it legally. This section even allows a cyclist to use the far left lane if it is a one-way street with more than two lanes.

Cyclists cannot ride more than two abreast. This takes up more roadway than is deemed prudent. A few cycling clubs ought to post this law on the doorway of the clubhouse and require all club members to read and understand it before going out as a group!

Cyclists must learn to use proper hand signals. A left turn

> "The world speed record on a bicycle is held by John Howard of the US. In 1985 he reached 154 mph (245 km/h), cycling in the slipstream of a specially designed car."
> —www.didyouknow.org/bicycles.htm

is indicated by the left arm sticking straight out. A right turn is indicated by extending the left hand and arm up above the bicycle.

Cyclists should learn that motorists cannot see their right arm extended straight out to indicate a right turn. A stop is indicated by extending the left hand downward and revealing a flat hand. Cyclists should also be in the habit of keeping at least one hand on the handlebar. Your personal safety is at stake here; the lights and reflectors increase the chance of being seen by a motorist. In spite of the fact that some cyclists can ride without their hands on the bars, the practice is extremely risky.

Cyclists using a sidewalk or bicycle pathway will travel at a prudent speed and keep the bicycle under control. Many municipalities don't allow bikes on the sidewalks for safety reasons. I often prefer to ride on the roadways and avoid the bicycle paths because of this. Experienced cyclists (who should know better) ignore the common sense behind the law and simply go where they want, even passing other cyclists into oncoming bike traffic. I've seen too many cyclists pushed off the path or collide head on because of this arrogance.

The laws for cars and bikes seem to be based on common sense. Many people, however, abandon common sense the second they are behind a wheel or on a bicycle. Our country reduced death and injury related to automobile accidents by governing speed and vehicular activity, and also by educating future drivers. It is now mandatory to complete a driver-education course before being able to apply for a driver's license. While there are few who would advocate bicycle operators' licenses, many would advocate bicycle-operator education.

Ibike.org lists several ideas for educational programs they believe would contribute to a reduction in automobile/bicycle and bicycle accidents. They call it the Bicycle Safety Education program; its intent is to reduce injury.

The program ideas are fairly comprehensive and worthy of some review.

Start with fourth-graders across the country (and even pick up fifth- and sixth-grade students) and provide them with comprehensive bicycle safety training.

In conjunction with bike shops, provide helmet safety information and provide discount coupons on helmets.

Working through the local PTAs, educate parents on topics of safe cycling that apply not only to their children but also to themselves. The assumption is that if the parents ride safely, so will the child.

The plan goes on to include:

- Incorporating bicycle safety into the curriculum of Parks and Recreation day camps;

- Incorporating awareness of laws governing bicycles on the roadway into high school driver-training curricula;

- Encouraging (and possibly financing) bicycle rodeos through local police departments;

- Issuing regular press releases regarding the benefits of wearing helmets and safe riding to small local presses in need of content (this has always been an effective grassroots method of getting news out for all types of political organizations);

- Promote regular radio and television interviews with local celebrities who believe in bicycling. Imagine if just one of the three Americans who have won the Tour de France would speak to motorists and cyclists about safety on the roads!

Under the enforcement section, ibike.org advocates that local law enforcement begin to cite adults (and even children) *at least* with warnings, and mandate attendance at bicycle safety workshops in lieu of fines. Bicycle police squads could be dispatched to monitor activity on urban trails, as they do in Seattle, and warn cyclists that they must wear a helmet in the city or face stiff penalties.

All of these ideas are sound and probably would serve the best interests of citizens, raise the awareness of safety among both motorists and cyclists, and enforce the laws equally; in addition, there's a strong provision for quality education on safety. I called the office of a King County, Washington, council member and spoke to a staffer. She said these and other suggestions have been floated as possible curbs to bicycle-related accidents, but in the end what they usually say is, "show me the money."

Local bicycle clubs can often pick up the slack. The Birmingham Bicycle Club of Birmingham, Alabama, hosts a website promoting its club activities. Among them is an annual League of American Bicyclists-sponsored class lasting twelve to fourteen hours and including both classroom and road instruction. The site claims the class is based on the premise that bicyclists fare better when they "act and are treated as motor vehicles." Students are taught effective skills for riding in traffic and how to handle situations they encounter on the road.

The website for the Great Plains Bicycle Club of Lincoln, Nebraska, includes a well-researched page on bicycle safety with the words "Wear a Helmet" prominent on the page. It lists several safety tips and discounts the notion that it's always safer to ride on the sidewalk. The safety links provided are informative and effective.

The Bikes Not Bombs program in Boston focuses on several programs, most importantly the Summer Youth Bicycle Safety and Mechanics Program and the more serious Teen Vocational Training Program. Participants in these programs take part in the Earn a Bike program, in which children are allowed to earn a bike by helping to fix it; in the process, they receive basic safety information. Older teens receive valuable formal and hands-on training as employable bicycle mechanics.

In one way or another, all three of these safety programs provide the community with much-needed safety training, primarily for children but also for adults, with the intent of making cycling safer. Obviously, it would benefit any community if the local bike club undertook these activities, and this is more easily done if there is financial and logistical support from club members.

Workshops and clinics that focus on handling skills are very important for beginning cyclists. The most important skills for beginning and intermediate cyclists should include information on safe speeds, correct turning, riding with other cyclists, and riding in traffic. (In the next chapter, I'll look at theories of urban planning for bicycles. This chapter will handle in depth some of the issues pertaining to the creation of bicycle paths and trails that encourage cycling. For now, I just want to keep the focus on safe riding.)

Most seasoned cyclists complain openly about dedicated trails and paths where they try to maintain the safe allowable speed of ten to fifteen miles an hour. The paths become either a raceway for training at speeds in excess of twenty-five miles an hour, or an open space where children are encouraged to ride slowly, weaving across the path onto the grass and then back onto the path. Cyclists training for racing should find open roads and streets for this purpose. Families wishing to start children out on bicycles should honestly gauge the level of activity on any given path and find an area where other children are allowed to ride freely. Mixing three levels of cyclists on one type of path is a recipe for serious injury.

It seems obvious enough to suggest that cyclists practice a standard rule of the motorway: keep to the right unless passing safely. Countless times I have encountered adult cyclists either weaving to both sides of a path, or passing directly into oncoming cyclists. I am not sure of the reasoning behind this. Do they expect other cyclists to stop and allow them to pass? That is usually not the case. Most cyclists keep to their right and wait for a clear shot before passing.

Children should be encouraged to ride their bikes at the earliest age possible. They should be taught the bicycle operates at peak efficiency when it moves relatively straight, following the curve of the road. Too many children are allowed to ride in whatever direction they choose. Unfortunately this is often not corrected as the child grows and starts riding the bike to school, weaving in and out of traffic, crossing streets in the middle of a block without looking, and failing to yield or stop when appropriate. The outcome is often injury or even death.

Turning is a skill that even the most ardent racers need to practice regularly. At slow speeds, turns are usually very manageable. Increase the speed, and the cyclist needs to start considering the line he or she will need to safely navigate. There are some tight, narrow corners on the Burke Gilman trail in Seattle, and head-on accidents occur frequently because inexperienced cyclists do not consider what will happen when they approach a turn at a high rate of speed with the wrong geometric line. They find themselves in the other lane, either forcing the oncoming cyclist off the path or suffering a direct hit.

Turning on city streets in the company of automobiles must also be taught and practiced correctly. Motorists are usually not aware of cyclists. If they are aware of anything, they are looking at other cars, especially the car in front of them. A cyclist can be guaranteed frequent potential hazards when riding with moving automobiles, especially when cornering. The motorist often is not aware of—or really does not want—the bicycle on the street. All of this adds up to a scenario that can easily result in serious injury or death, usually suffered by the cyclist.

A retired couple living near my former home in Kingston, Washington, were lifelong cyclists. He raced and she rode more than a thousand miles a month during her commuting years. They knew how to handle their bikes. Admittedly, as they grew older, their reflexes were not as sharp, and they didn't look forward to the years when they would need to curb their desire for long rides on open country roads, especially as traffic followed a growing population.

This was ultimately what killed them as they rode into the city of Poulsbo: the driver of a pickup truck approached them from behind, honking his horn loudly with long blasts. The oncoming traffic in the other lane was not yielding and the truck driver was not going to slow: he wanted the cyclists off the road. Both of them were trained to avoid this kind of danger by heading at an acute angle safely into the ditch or bushes. The noise of the horn frightened the man, however, and rather than angling toward the ditch, he swerved into the path of the pickup truck; his wife hit his bike and was pulled under the truck.

This tragic event happens too frequently in every state. The cause of these deaths is a combination of criminal driving on the part of the driver and lack of proper skill and precaution on the part of the cyclists. The intent of this book is not to frighten people away from cycling, but to encourage safe cycling.

Before we proceed into other cycling considerations, I want to make one point very clear: *ride safely*!

THREE

Getting Fit for Longer Rides

> Bicycle riding as little as three miles a day
> will improve your sex life.
>
> —DR. FRANCO ANTONINI

The easy part of cycling is the actual riding, unless you ride out of Boulder straight up into the Rockies. But once you have the right bike under you, and you are aware of basic safety precautions, the rest is fairly simple. It is important to remember that getting fit really makes you feel good: you have more energy, more stamina, and a brighter outlook.

It is equally important to remember to take it easy. Even the most seasoned racers start with something relatively straight forward.

In *Fear and Loathing in Las Vegas*, gonzo journalist Hunter S. Thompson described his preparations for a road trip; they included stocking his car with copious amounts of drugs and alcohol. This makes for entertaining reading, but my own journey requires a different preparation.

Beat writer Jack Kerouac claimed to have written *On the Road* in a record twenty-two days; in it he describes a journey that begins to become spiritual in nature. He set a standard for using the metaphor of a journey as a device to describe a reflection on spiritual growth.

Perhaps he borrowed a literary device from Geoffrey Chaucer, the acclaimed author of *The Canterbury Tales*, a literary account of a pilgrimage to the Holy Land. Noteworthy in the *Tales* is a constant reference to the physical effort required to make the journey, as well as the material preparations necessary to ensure proper diet and rest.

These three divergent writers saw the relationship between spiritual growth and the journey. They also took pains to get ready for the long haul.

I know athletes who use long-distance running as their vehicle for taking the actual journey. If they stop training over a nasty winter, the first two months of decent weather are spent carefully reconditioning. I found it necessary to go through this same process each spring and finally decided it was worth suffering through the foul winter rains of Seattle; now I ride twelve months of the year and stay in consistent physical condition.

To illustrate the need for physical fitness on the kind of journey I have chosen to undertake, allow me a brief story. My sister Mary and I both went to visit my brother in Kingston, Washington. The three of us planned a Sunday morning ride over a thirty-mile course that took us mostly up steep hills and down sharp inclines. It was not flat, and I was not in shape.

In terms used by racing enthusiasts, I was dropped. About eighteen miles into the ride, they disappeared. I caught up to them at the house after they had showered and were eating lunch. I can honestly say I have never been that badly conditioned since. I learned a most valuable lesson.

At the time, I just figured I was out of shape. At twenty-eight, the solution is easy, right? Get the sweats on, jog a bit, throw some weights around and get on the bike. I know now I was on the verge of developing sarcopenia. Even at twenty-eight, this is relatively easy to do. I noticed an advertisement focused on professionals in their late twenties and early thirties who were having a difficult time keeping up with their profession and staying in shape. That precisely describes me at that age, pursuing my MBA as well as managing new construction projects in Seattle.

This is the condition we suffer as we age and decrease our physical activity. It is measured by a loss of muscle mass and, in most cases, an increase of fat tissue to replace it. This is often referred to as *going soft*. Our body size may not increase noticeably for several years unless we are totally out of control with the doughnuts and milkshakes. But the muscle tissue declines and the fat tissue increases. We are therefore unable to function as we once did.

This condition is not reserved for the middle-aged; anyone in their twenties can suffer from it, the result of prolonged periods of physical inactivity. There are as many remedies as there are web-sites explaining the condition. Some doctors, nutritionists, and personal trainers prescribe a wide range of remedies, from increased physical activity to drugs to strict diets. I am not sure what the sure cure is; I can only speak to my experience.

I got back on my bike. I tried a long ride first time out, recalling my peak fitness years when I could easily ride more than one hundred miles in a day. I got as far as thirty miles out and was in so much pain I was crying on the side of the road. I caught a series of buses and made my way home, only to sit in the bathtub and local YMCA Jacuzzi for several days until I recovered.

I do not suffer from this anymore. I can ride more than one hundred miles in a single day, and I do not ignore opportunities to get some exercise, whether aerobic or for strength training.

Let's approach the subject of going soft honestly, especially if physical activity is going to be an integral part of a personal improvement plan. The recipe for going soft is easy. Just stop exercising and use any one of thousands of excuses to get home, pour out a drink, eat dinner and watch television until late and go to bed. Do this for three or four months and you will go soft. I am not in a position to say at what point sarcopenia sets in, but if this pattern continues, it will.

Christian theologians tell me two things. First, I was made in the image and likeness of God and, second, I am the temple of the Holy Spirit. I have no intention of disputing either assertion, since I can neither prove nor disprove them. For the sake of argument, let's assume they're both true.

Being created in God's image and likeness is acceptable, knowing that when I take over as a consenting adult, I can do literally anything I want to this body. It might be the wrong thing, but it's my choice.

It's the temple part that perplexes me. Does it mean that my heart and soul should reflect the Holy Spirit? Or is it more literal, my entire being is a temple, including my body? If this belief includes my entire being, then why do so many believers do so many bad things to their bodies?

The obvious extremes are various forms of substance abuse. Not only do drugs block the mind and heart from reaching any level of awareness or true happiness, they destroy the body. A less serious extreme is obesity. I am speaking here of a condition that is beyond simple sarcopenia. I am speaking of habitual overeating of foods that clog arteries and constantly increase fat.

The story of a close friend is relevant: he has been living through various stages of AIDS for fifteen years, and with some very good medication is managing to maintain a life that is relatively healthy and most definitely happy. He attributes part of this to his daily cycling. He's not a Christian, but he certainly appreciates his life and body and his ability to feel bliss and pain on the same ride. He is determined to keep his body as healthy as possible; it was a gift that was being destroyed, and he now wants to take care of as if it were a golden vessel.

This is easy when we are young; it gets increasingly difficult as we age. My own recovery after a long period without regular and focused exercise is now more than twice as long as it was at nineteen. And there are the risks associated with trying to kick-start a body gone to seed.

The President's Council on Aging offers some good advice on how to approach regaining some level of physical fitness, either at an older age or after an injury. The advice comes from a variety of sources and comments first on the physical changes we experience as our bodies age. There will be a normal decrease in the maximum heart rate, thereby limiting the level of physical activity. Lung capacity will decrease, which will result in a decrease in strength and endurance. Finally reaction time diminishes as the flow of blood to the brain decreases.

If this were happening to my car, I would start looking for a trade-in!

I have worked hard to delay these symptoms and have been successful so far. I am fortunate to enjoy the very exercise that is also at the core of my spiritual practice.

For most people, the process of recovering heart rate and lung and nervous system capacity is within relatively easy reach. It's not necessary to maintain an extremely high level of fitness over an entire life, although that is advisable. If it is necessary to recapture physical fitness, the most important step is the first one.

It is recommended that the first step be an easy one, and definitely one informed by your physician. The American Heart Association also recommends an exercise that is rhythmic—one with pattern and repetition. The rhythm is slow at first, and increases over time, as rapidly as the individual can master. The association recommends fun activities that will bring some joy and happiness as well as health to one's life. This will also counteract the tedium some people experience when exercising. Finally, in addition to drinking plenty of water during your regimen, they recommend longer warm-ups and cool-downs to encourage elasticity in the muscles.

This all appears to be common sense. Actually, these recommendations are widely distributed for free precisely because many people do not observe them. Take care to make a recovery exercise plan effective by taking it slowly at first, and then be as aggressive as necessary. Staying fit or getting back in shape comes with some inherent pain. It is more intense at first, less intense later, but it never goes away.

What remains unanswered is why endure the pain.

In some demented fashion, I enjoy the pain: the rewards far exceed the effort. I do not have the internal peace or a sense of wholeness if I cannot ride easily for an hour or more. Trying to do this once or twice a year without any serious plan to maintain a high level of fitness would be detrimental. If we know our bodies, we know why this is true. Unused muscles need to be strengthened slowly.

I often wonder if there isn't some real spiritual benefit from enduring pain. I don't think it is the pain *per se* that brings the benefit, though. It is the triumph over the pain: the moment when the pain subsides, and I am more physically capable than before. I accept the pain as inevitable and most assuredly do not pursue it as an end. But I do feel better when I can overcome the pain, either at the moment it occurs or over time as I become more fit. I advise new cyclists to try and reach a deeper understanding of their own capacity by understanding how they deal with the pain.

Other cyclists I know, and some interviewed for this book, laughed at the question regarding pain. Pain is inevitable. Traffic is inevitable. Rain is inevitable (at least in Seattle!). Cycling allows me to face up to those inevitable problems and experience them in a way I cannot experience them in a car. People scratch their heads, but I long ago gave up trying to explain exactly why that grind up the four-mile-long hill is actually a good thing. I really enjoy the deep sense of accomplishment when I get to the top and roll down the other side.

I am careful to differentiate the "pain" I feel trying to get back in shape after being a couch potato all winter from the real physical pain someone feels after an accident. The pain I feel is transitory and quite easily managed, while the pain that follows an accident or as a result of disease is a completely different topic. If I sound courageous facing up to a few cramped muscles with a stiff upper lip, I cannot promise I would react the same way if I were suffering from cancer.

Notwithstanding that, pain is a challenge. I know the pain diminishes as I increase my fitness. When I have achieved something I call my own optimum fitness, I hardly notice the pain and enjoy more the feeling of muscles doing what they were actually designed to do.

I put this topic in any consideration of cycling because attacking a hill without proper fitness can not only be painful—but can be harmful, as well. If you are not in shape, start slowly and believe that in good measure you will also enjoy the feeling of muscles doing what they were designed to do.

FOUR

Carbohydrates Are Our Friends

Small portions are for small, inactive people

—JIM HARRISON *JUST BEFORE DARK*

One of the first discoveries new cyclists make, and one that seasoned cyclist prepare for, is the amount of energy exerted cycling. On one afternoon ride around Vashon Island near Seattle, we burned over four thousand calories. That's a lot of food! Now that you are on this cycling journey, get ready to really crave food, and lots of it.

During the recent low-carb diet craze, I shocked people by buying food that actually had large amounts of complex carbohydrates. My stated mission was to weigh more, and the diet freaks wagged their tongues and shook their heads. Conventional wisdom demanded that I reduce carbs and my weight. Instead, I loaded up on carbs, gained weight, and reduced my waist by two sizes.

The weight gain was in increased muscle mass.

I was raised to use my body to get things done. I never lifted weights so I cannot comment on what it must feel like to be divinely sculpted, but I do know what it is like to be strong. I didn't become strong by avoiding carbohydrates. I have always eaten enough food to be strong, but not to become overweight.

As I completed a bachelor's degree and two master's degrees, I noticed my grades were good when I maintained my strength, and I needed to eat to maintain the strength. When I was in graduate school I was known to always have a pot of spaghetti on the stove and some drinkable red wine available. Fellow students—who'd never had to fend for themselves—would stop by to "study" and help themselves to plates full of carbohydrates. Of course, during that time I also was cycling upward of one hundred miles a week.

My niece recently accumulated many of my mother's favorite recipes from note pads, scraps of paper, and her memory, and produced a nice cookbook as a Christmas gift. I am including some of those recipes in Appendix One, and they're useful for cyclists, especially the carb-loaded ones. I grew up eating food now considered sinful, and I often looked as though I wasn't being fed. In fact, I was eating more than most men when I was fifteen. And, again, I was also cycling, skiing, playing soccer, and working for my father's construction company on the weekends.

I am not even an amateur dietician, but I am smart enough to know food is fuel for strength if used properly. If I am going to continue using cycling as a spiritual practice—and I will—I need to eat. I also know, from still wearing the same size of jeans I wore in high school, that diets do not need to be the *best possible* diet to be a *very good* diet. I have eaten my share of bad food and occasionally have drunk too much alcohol. I eat birthday cake, Christmas cookies, pork rinds, potato chips, and drink chocolate milk. I eat red meat and pork. I also eat a lot of raw fruit and vegetables, fish, nuts, whole-grain bread, rice, milk, juice, and eggs. Most important, I eat a lot and not gain weight and my blood pressure stays consistently around one-twenty-eight over eighty-eight.

Food fuels my cycling, and cycling increases my desire for food. It is a part of my preparation for a long ride. During the ride, I eat whatever I like, and when the ride is finished, I eat again. If bicycling can be considered a spiritual exercise, food is a very important part of that. Without a lot of good food, cycling would be detrimental to my health.

What is amazing is that cycling causes food to *taste* better as well. Any food! Even poorly cooked or usually bad-tasting food goes down with delight. Twinkies, greasy doughnuts, fast food . . . it all goes down fine. I think this is where I need to discipline myself. My appetite is voracious during and after a long ride. The fast food joints give me satisfaction quickly, and buying components of a meal yet to be cooked usually discourages me from doing that. I need to plan ahead.

Cooking up pots of spaghetti and freezing them ensures that I get something really good for me in relatively short time. Keeping a refrigerator stocked with raw fruits and vegetables begins to satisfy the craving. Cheese and breads add substance. I write this because I know some cyclists who don't keep a stock of good food and resort to the fast-food trick as they wind down and head for home. Yes, they are skinny and look healthy, but we can all hide from our bad habits for a while. They will eventually catch up to us.

This is where my discussion with friends and food lovers becomes complex. People make individual choices about the food they eat. There are many divergent factions that believe it necessary to convince people to eat or not eat certain types of food. My doctor wants me to eat less salt and sugar, and I see the need for that. Other people scold me for eating murdered animals; they decry the torturous methods used to slaughter millions of creatures every year and tell me there is real pain in this process. Others want me to look at food from the specifically theological perspective and see eating as a means of gaining sanctity.

An argument was made to me showing the value of a meatless diet for cycling, that it actually improved performance. I follow professional cycling very closely and without revealing names, I am familiar with the training diets and the food served during large stage tours to many of the most elite cyclists in the world—and these diets include red meat.

I want to avoid that argument because, like most arguments, it usually goes nowhere. If people elect not to eat meat, I support that choice, as much as I would support the choice my friends make to invite me to a barbeque featuring a select cut of beef.

I wanted to acknowledge this concern people have, and in turn want to appreciate that many people will eat red meat as an important staple of their diet. They feel the protein is important and generally like the flavor. In short, food is so important to cycling, I do not want there to be any argument, just an enjoyment of the practice.

I have to eat; there is no question that I must eat after a long ride. Where and with whom I eat is the focus of the rest of this chapter.

I am perfectly content eating alone, particularly when my blood sugar is low as a result of very strenuous exercise. I am a grouch when I have not eaten properly. I eat what is necessary to stabilize and improve my disposition and only then am I allowed to be with other people! I have made more verbal blunders in this condition than I have ever made while drinking. Friends know: if Shawn is hungry, leave him alone.

Once the emergency passes, I love a food party. People try to drag me out to nightclubs and late-night parties, and I can shrug my shoulders and walk away. But suggest a new restaurant or a seven-course dinner party, and I'm there.

My approach to eating is that of celebration, and it's enhanced because I am always hungry. I enjoy eating and then in turn have fuel to ride, which ends up making me hungry, and I stop in for Mexican or pub food.

I am an easy target for someone in need of a decent meal. When I was teaching, students would join in, two or three at a time, because they knew I liked good food and would usually pay. I got feedback from students on their coursework and progress reports on projects, and they got a free meal. And I never had a bad time doing this.

My family is large, huge to some. I have eleven brothers and sisters, twenty-six nieces and nephews, and now twelve great-nieces and nephews. And there are numerous spouses. We have even acquired non-blood-related family members who started out as friends and showed up at our events often enough that they just became family!

We gather as often as we can and while it's rare that everyone make the event, usually there are twenty or more and the food is potluck. There are salads, hams, desserts, salmon, cooked vegetable dishes, cookies, wine . . . and my brother-in-law owns part of a brewery, so there's usually a keg. This is for any kind of event, like a birthday or Mother's Day. We usually ride a fifteen-mile loop near my brother's house and then eat. And eat. Then drink some beer and eat some more.

Where I work, we show appreciation to students at least four times a year by barbecuing hamburgers (meat and vegetarian), and supplying enough food to feed a small battalion. We eat over two days, so all students have a chance to get at least one meal out of us, and they usually show up for all four servings! Prospective students visit the school and enjoy four different kinds of pizza . . . and since I am a part of the recruiting process, explaining some of the degree programs, they invite me to eat—and I accept.

I studied the Catholic Eucharistic celebration, commonly known as the mass, extensively while in the seminary. Mass is a celebration memorializing the Last Supper. I see very little difference between groups gathering to celebrate a birthday or to welcome students back into school and this celebration.

I was invited to a Sunday dinner at a Hare Krishna community in Denver. One of the members was a student of mine in computer programming and, after numerous invitations, I accepted. While the food was different and delightful, it had all of the markings of a Catholic mass. We were formally welcomed, they read from their scripture, we passed food around and sang songs, and there was a formal departure.

The diner parties I attend with literary friends are modeled much the same way. There is a formal welcome of each attendee, we read from our own work or from that of some famous author, we eat, and then we leave.

There is no mystery in the fact that the Last Supper was a Jewish Seder meal. The integration of people gathering and eating and a spiritual celebration upon reflection seems quite natural. Even die-hard atheists who claim there is no deity of any kind are drawn into eating as spiritual celebration. While they may not understand the physical machinations of a celebration as highly defined as the Mass, they still participate in celebrations that are extremely similar in ritual.

I rarely consider food a simple physical nourishment. It could be a spiritual exercise in its own right, but I consider it a cornerstone of my own spiritual practices. Finally, however, there is always a human-interest story to be told about food, especially among cyclists. On an easy Sunday morning ride at almost race pace, we spent nearly two hours in the saddle and burned more than two thousand calories. We ate before, during, and after the ride, and later that evening I was still hungry.

To determine what foods are really good, we can go to the world's greatest chefs and ask what they think. I always believe that if the chef is rotund and happy, I want to eat her food. If the chef is wafer thin, I want to smell his food first and pick at the edges until I can understand why he doesn't eat.

After the chef, there are the cyclists. Knowing they need to eat excessively more than most people, I want to know what it is they eat.

I found some websites that gave me some insight. First, the site run by the Bay Area Velo Girls, "the San Francisco Bay area's premier cycling club for women and girls." The bios of the members include bits of information about them, the most interesting being how they responded to the question of "favorite post-ride treat." It's an interesting list that includes dried bananas, buckwheat pancakes, scrambled eggs, chicken apple sausage, copious amounts of coffee, decaf Café Feddo with whipped cream, margaritas, burritos, peanut-butter builders bar, and chocolate.

Food Facts

- Bananas (per 126g serving): 110kcal, 0g fat, 29g carbohydrate of which sugars 21g.

- Mars Bar (per 65g serving): 11g fat, 44g carbohydrate (100% sugar), 293kcal.

- Dried fruits are also very good; they contain no fat for around 100kcal in 50g.

—Alexandre Lagache, www.biketrip.org/docs2.php?docid=28

I am a little surprised by the list; the culinary arts in the Bay Area offer such a wide variety of great cuisine, I'd have thought they could do a little better than dried bananas! I never go through the Bay area without stopping for some really fresh sourdough bread and maybe drive an hour north for some Napa Valley wine.

The Haul'N Ass Race Team of Denver, Colorado, posts the bios of their racers. They were asked simply to name their favorite food. This list includes "anything with taurine;" a homemade concoction of grains, seeds, nuts and fruit for cereal; garlic with some pasta; Fat Tire Ale; Swanky's Fish and Chips with a side order of mac-

and-cheese; maple nut oatmeal; onion rings; euro pastries; Guinness; fajitas; chipotle; kielbasa; French cooking; and a long and assorted list of energy and protein drinks.

Now, this list from Denver (which I am guessing also includes some folks from Boulder) is more in tune with the local cuisine. When I lived in Boulder, there was always talk of food, but it was focused on food that was really good for you and did not upset the balance of nature.

Tri Sport Bicycles of Fresno, California, hosts a website listing the bios of employees. The list of post-ride favorite foods among sales people and mechanics includes: shrimp tacos from anywhere, grilled chicken sandwich from the Dam Diner, burrito, forty-ounce malt liquor, burritos, anything free, pizza, Mojo Fries from the North Folk Shell Station, Olive Garden Chicken Gardino, Guinness extra stout, and one of my favorites, Marshmallow Peeps.

The men and women of the University of Idaho Cycling Team list these favorites as "bonk food." They include waffles, cheese and eggs, toast, Snickers, and Coke.

The women and men of Whitman College call their favorite foods "the breakfast of champions," and they eat carrots and spinach, apples, Raisin Bran with banana, yogurt and pineapple, Grape-nuts mixed with raisin bran, granola with yogurt, a "Mr. Ed" from Gunsmoke, blueberry buckwheat pancakes with real maple syrup, banana pancakes and, among other items, a heaping plate of cheese quesadillas, and a gallon of Walla Walla's finest wine. Take note, the Whitman Cycling Team of Walla Walla won the 2006 Collegiate Nationals. Maybe there is something in the wine.

Some of the cyclists who listed their favorite foods also listed the dietary supplements they use. These are typically not banned substances and racing authorities have no qualms about their use. According to Melvin Williams, Ph.D., there are unscrupulous manufacturers and dealers of dietary supplements who will include banned substances. In my review of favorite foods and the dietary supplements, cyclists always mentioned off-the-shelf products that meet all the legal criteria.

Dr. Williams authored a series of six articles on the effects of dietary supplements on performance. His conclusions were consistent with my own unscientific experiences: food tastes better and offers the same performance enhancements as legal dietary supplements. Somehow pasta, green salad, fresh apricots, tomatoes, blueberry buckwheat pancakes with real maple syrup and bananas sounds so much better than consuming a paste of gritty lab-generated vitamins and minerals!

I reaffirmed my awareness of how important food is to cyclists in writing this book. I thought I was the only person to suffer from low blood sugar and get cranky. Cycling will definitely increase the need for food, and it will also increase the desire for any food. In chapter thirteen, in an interview with members of bike4peace, one member notes just how fun it is to consume foods that are traditionally considered bad, knowing tomorrow we will ride another ten or fifty miles and burn all the harmful fats and sugars away!

Now that we've established the importance of fitness and food, we begin to examine how people grow deeper into cycling. This is progressive, and will end for everyone at the point they choose, some making ultimate commitments to cycling while others are perfectly satisfied with short weekend trips. The bottom line, however, is that cycling reacquaints us with the joy of food.

FIVE

Bicycling Is All the Rage

Peace begins with a smile.

—Mother Teresa

The reality of road rage hits the news every day. My intent in considering it here is to explore options for minimizing its impact on cyclists. Sam Adams, Commissioner of Transportation for the City of Portland, posted a response to comments made on a syndicated radio program heard by thousands of Portlanders. The comments were directed at cyclists, and quoting the Sam Adams website, were to the effect of, "when I hear on TV that a cyclist has been and killed by a car, I laugh; I think it's funny," and, "if you are a cyclists, you should know I exist, that I don't care about you. That I don't care about your life."

Commissioner Adams pointed out his right to free speech, but differentiated it from other language used on the radio program that incites violence.

More interesting than Commissioner Adam's original response to this was the reaction by anti-cycling citizens. Someone named Anthony wrote this:

Wow, Sam.

I think I understand the point of the 95.5 broadcast.

The city, state, and even feds have made many people believe that bicycles are the equivalent to a 2,000-plus lb. car. They (meaning you) constantly tell us it's an "alternative" to driving and they do everything they possibly can to promote this "alternative."

Fact is, motor vehicles are larger, heavier, and travel much faster then any bicycle, yet they are expected to share the road. Since bikes are more maneuverable then cars, most bicyclists ignore major traffic laws (like stopping at a stop sign). This only multiplies the problem.

Bicycles and motor vehicles do not mix. ANY person dumb enough to take a bicycle out into fast moving traffic (including the un-used bike lanes on the east side) is just asking to be killed.

In Lakewood, Colorado, a cyclist was shot to death by the driver of a pickup truck. Police described it as road rage. In Seattle, members of Critical Mass were arrested not by the Seattle Police, but by undercover King County deputies returning from their fieldwork; the cyclists of the Critical Mass had even blocked the intersection and the deputies took it upon themselves the make the arrests. The incident focused attention on a practice that many motorists find excessively irritating: cyclists intentionally blocking traffic during rush hour on Friday afternoons.

Research libraries and numerous websites offer examples and explanations of road rage. The Online Journal of Peace and Reconciliation notes what they believe are the causes of road rage. The stated intent of the website is to foster peace where there often is a lack of peace. We want to think of cycling as a recreation or sport that is relaxing, or competitive in a healthy way, but when aggressive drivers and passive cyclists cross paths, the ultimate goal is to avoid conflict and to achieve a sense of personal peace.

I read the content of this website with great interest. I am aware

Identifying the Causes of Road Rage

1. Congestion of highways, roadways, and streets. Rising urban and suburban populations significantly increase the number of cars.

2. A rise in interpersonal and intrapersonal stress stemming from job- and family-related issues.

3. Listening to loud music while driving.

4. The need to save face and overcome feelings of being disrespected.

5. The need to assert identity and control.

6. A cultural focus on time, saving it, and using it wisely.

7. A human need for space, causing drivers to become territorial.

8. The summer heat.

9. A breakdown in manners.

10. A cultural focus on masculinity and machismo.

11. A "me first" mentality.

12. Oppressive social conditions leading to feelings of alienation.

13. Defensive driving skills that focus attention on a perceived lack of driving skills in others.

14. Increased sense of invincibility in larger vehicles.

of the fact that there are motorists who are impatient, and since cycling is a part of my spiritual exercises, I need to find a way of minimizing negative or aggressive encounters.

This list is part of an article entitled "The Phenomenon of Road Rage: Complexities, Discrepancies and Opportunities for CR Analysis" by K. Michelle Scott.

The list includes several more "causes," some which I found implausible, such as "lower emotional intelligence and moral character" and "increased immigration trends leading to a mixture of different driving styles." The site is by its own admission unscientific and does not claim any verifiable proof of any of the listed reasons for road rage. But gut instinct tells us many of them are probably correct. Road rage is an irrational behavior that, if directed toward cyclists, normally adversely affects the cyclist and not the automobile.

The site suggests possible solutions: Increased driver education, anger management therapy, increased law enforcement, and intelligent transportation devices that ultimately increase efficient use of the highways.

The Colorado State Patrol reports receiving an average of one hundred and seventy-one reports of road rage each day. They are quick to point out that the people engaged in this behavior are of all ages, races, genders, and socio-economic classes. There is no one kind of person who engages in road rage. The state patrol campaign includes patrolling for aggressive drivers before the situation escalates into road rage, and citing drivers for following too closely, aggressively cutting across lanes, and swerving without properly signaling.

The OJPCR site suggests using the conflict framework proposed by Terrell Northrup in *From Identity to Escalation*. The book lists four stages of conflict:

1. Threat

2. Distortion

3. Ridgification

4. Collusion where the conflict is incorporated into each person's identification.

Aside from the suggested solutions offered on the OJPCR site, there are strategies a cyclist can use to minimize exposure to road rage. When we understand what irritates a motorist, we can possibly avoid aggravating this irritation. Some strategies might include using only designated bicycle paths until we are able to maintain the same speed as cars on the street. Another strategy might include never using aggressive tactics like weaving through traffic, causing motorists to slam brakes and horns. An acceptable strategy is not, however, hanging the bike up in the garage and driving!

I will note in the next chapter the type of urban planning used in Denver, Colorado, to achieve this goal: allowing enough space for cars and bicycles so there is less conflict between the two modes of transportation. If a pickup truck can pass a cyclist freely because there's enough room for both, the occurrences of road rage will diminish. It won't disappear; many motorists are simply opposed to the presence of cyclists and will never welcome them, no matter how wide the street is.

If there is no urban plan in place, there are other strategies. Drivers (including me when I drive) tend to use arterials and highways to commute to work. Commuting times are hectic because no one ever leaves early enough to drive slowly to work. Most municipalities offer maps of roadways for cyclists where various colors are used based on traffic counts. Roads and streets that are red might indicate high levels of commuting traffic, while green might indicate lower or nonexistent commuting traffic. These are often coordinated with designated paths so a route can be selected that would include a combination of low traffic streets, designated paths, and wider shoulders.

Cyclists in training for competitive racing can drive out to more remote areas where the highways are less traveled. Forcing the issue of the cyclists right to the roadway by riding in large groups through the city might be an effective demonstration and when coordinated with the local municipality can be safe and effective.

But it's a form of belligerence to ride in a pack through city streets at less than posted speeds, blocking traffic in both directions. This would get an angry response even from me, and it happens too frequently. In my chapter on rules of the road, I list one of Seattle's laws that does not permit cyclists to ride more than two abreast. Observing the law, even as a cyclist, is one strategy for reducing road rage.

Positive advocacy can result in positive change. The League of American Bicyclists' website offers a comprehensive list of action plans and organizational tips for positive local advocacy. It is in the best interest of all municipalities to reduce single-occupancy automobile commuting. Reducing traffic also reduces congestion and damage to the roadways. Advocating for designated paths, streets with traffic-calming devices, streets designated for cyclists only, and comprehensive regional planning can lead to safer cycling. The League website is adamant about positive public relations, which always includes courteous communications and active participation in planning.

One cyclist who has suffered numerous negative encounters with drivers proposed to buy a handgun in the near future. I don't think opening your heart to something like cycling includes carrying a handgun during high-stress commuting times!

SIX

If We Build a Path, Will They Ride?

After your first day of cycling, one dream is inevitable.
A memory of motion lingers in the muscles of your legs, and
round and round they seem to go. You ride through Dreamland
on wonderful dream bicycles that change and grow.

—H.G. WELLS, *THE WHEELS OF CHANCE*

In the previous chapter, I mentioned the federal mandate to reduce single-occupancy vehicle trips, and noted how some municipalities view cyclists. Bicyclists are, to many city engineers, a nuisance. Cyclists, however, are a reality in every city in this country, and in growing numbers. Every major city has adopted some plan to accommodate alternative transportation, and this includes cycling. Most cities and highly populated counties issue, usually for free, maps highlighting safer bicycling routes into most work centers. These maps are available through municipal transportation offices, most bicycle shops, and typically on the website of the local county or city government.

There is a philosophy now among urban planners that not only welcomes cyclists, but embraces them. One in particular is the city of Denver. On the official city website is a copy of the 2003 revised master plan for bicycles. This is a comprehensive document brave enough to purposely incorporate bicycles and cars on the same streets, as well as continue to build and improve dedicated bicycle paths. The city planners plan for three types of cyclists:

- **The weekend and occasional family recreational rider.** These cyclists are out for a good time on a sunny day. They don't intend to ride more than five or ten miles an hour, ever, and will usually go short distances ranging from one to fifteen miles.

- **Daily commuters.** These cyclists ride anywhere from five to fifteen miles each way to and from work on a regular and consistent basis. Their ride needs to be fairly simple and definitely safe. If they are going to encounter automobiles, it has to be in a consistently safe environment to encourage more cyclists to ride.

- **Serious trainers and racers in training.** These cyclists want to ride longer distances at higher rates of speed, averaging between 20-35 miles per hour depending on the type of training.

Even though there might be a dedicated path for cyclists, there is also the need to "share the path" with people at all levels of cycling and walking skills. The Burke Gilman Trail near Seattle also allows for horses. This requires cyclists to use caution at every turn. The best rule of thumb is to observe the rules of the road, keep to the right unless passing, not ride at speeds that will cause accidents, not pass into blind corners, and not stop in the middle of the path to take pictures and chat. These might seem obvious tips, but a Sunday ride on any urban trail will reveal a number of these errors.

The 2003 plan has a place for everyone. In Denver, families can use the Washington Park loop, an easy two miles with a posted speed limit of fifteen miles per hour. While many training riders will exceed that speed, the park is still a great place for the weekend or occasional recreational rider. Planning includes a grid system throughout the city and roadways designed to have dedicated bicycle lanes in each direction. A map of the grid system demonstrates a commitment to making it easy and safe for cyclists to get from nearly any neighborhood in Denver to major work centers. It is obvious they do not believe the downtown corridor is the only work center; it is as easy to get to East Denver to work as it is downtown. Finally, training riders are encouraged to use the dedicated bicycle lanes at the posted speed to access the wider, less-used country roads that interconnect with the system and do their fast paced training away from the families and commuters.

Less comprehensive is the bicycle plan for the city of Seattle found on Seattle.gov, its website. The Seattle Bicycle Advisory Board section of the website boasts of twenty-eight miles of dedicated paths and over ninety miles of signed bicycle routes. I have ridden many of these routes often and find the markings often to be missing or very unclear. The white lines are fading as cars drive over them. There are some very popular routes (especially well-worn paths to the University of Washington) and not-so-well-traveled paths to the downtown core.

Boulder, Colorado, has a well-defined bicycle path system in something of a grid pattern. Using both street paths and dedicated pathways, it is very easy to commute to the University of Colorado and the widely diversified employment sections in the city. Most employers occupy a wide range of office parks peppered around Boulder County, with no main central business core.

The unique feature of the Boulder path system is the traffic-quieting efforts, especially on the high traveled paths within the city limits. The paths curve sharply and work around landscaping and decorative sculptures that serve to slow bicycle traffic out of respect for pedestrians and recreational cyclists.

Portland links users of the official city website to its bicycle program through a website with the URL of drivelesssavemore.com. The map of the bicycle paths and designated lanes costs six dollars and is not visible online. It's easier in Portland, however, to use more of a grid pattern than it is in Seattle. Portland is spread out in all directions and employment centers are located in all sections of the city. The trails and street paths allow cyclists to move from neighborhood to neighborhood with relative ease.

Boston has adopted a grid pattern for most of the downtown and areas around the universities, but the outlying areas still depend on moving toward the center and then back out to other neighborhoods. The city's comprehensive plan is focused on:

1. Safety education, training and public awareness

2. Traffic rules and enforcement

3. Bicycle transportation facilities

4. Bicycle parking and support facilities

5. Transit and intermodal connections

6. Bicycle promotion and tourism.

- Number of times cyclists forgot to take their bicycles off the bus: 353
- Time from University District to Pike Place Market:
  - Driving time in light traffic: 15 minutes
  - Driving time during rush hour: 35 minutes
  - Cycling time, moderate pace: 30 minutes
  - Time to park car: 5–25 minutes
  - Time to park and lock bike: 1 minute

—www.seattle.gov/transportation/bikeinfo.htm

Of particular interest are the transit and intermodal connections, something not clearly visible in other city bicycle plans. The plan incorporates the wide variety of public transportation modes available throughout the city. This makes the semi-grid system easier to navigate and use.

Boston also shows in its plan how streets should be marked in the future for bicycle paths, and the result is similar to that found in the revised master plan of 2003 for Denver. The city of Denver and some other cities have formed advocacy groups where citizens have a forum to advise government on the needs of cyclists. Ever major city has critical-path rides intended to raise awareness of the needs of cyclists, but the bulk of the advocacy in any city is going to be through larger, well-established bicycle clubs that have an interest in promoting cycling.

The bottom line, however, is no matter how much money a city spends on a bicycle plan, it is only as effective as the number of people who use it. I asked a group of parents of school-aged children if they encouraged or even allowed their kids to ride to school. The response was predominantly negative. In this truly unscientific poll, the most common reasons were concerns with safety, both physical safety and safety from predators. In response to these concerns, the parents had decided to drive their children to school.

One grade-school principal who wanted to speak off the record pined for the old days when the bikes racks were full, and there were no cars in front of the school. Now, the bike racks are empty or gone, and the cars line up in front of the school before and after sessions, often parked three abreast, causing neighborhood traffic jams. She said it was rare for children to ride their bikes to school on a consistent and regular basis.

A middle-school teacher sees the same thing. She is concerned, however, for a different reason. She will soon end her thirty-five year career and in the last ten years she has seen both a steady decline in the number of adolescents riding bikes to work and an equivalent rise in obesity. A few of her students participate in sports and—in spite of being driven to school—are active enough to stave off obesity but the students who would typically ride a bike to school now do nothing.

Perhaps to alleviate this fear, parents and schools can organize neighborhood groups of children riding bikes to school, much like the buddy system. Or, better yet, if time permits, parents can ride with their children to school and get some exercise in the process. My neighbors in Kingston were fortunate enough to have a home-based business and they rode the four miles to and from school every morning and afternoon, allowing some of the neighborhood children to ride with them.

For the last chapter of this book, I interviewed several people who have made a large or total commitment to the bike and, almost to the person, their first experience riding a bike was to and from school. Following on that mostly positive experience came a life-long commitment to the bike.

The urban planning noted in this chapter that focuses on bicycles, paths, designated streets, and education has been to serve an adult population commuting to work. My research did not reveal much to alleviate the trend toward dependence on the automobile because of concern for personal safety from both personal injury and from interference from predators.

Part of the ongoing challenge for urban planners is to develop bicycle plans that serve adults as well as children and adolescents, and that address the issues driving children away from the bicycle as a means of getting to school and forcing an increasing reliance on the family car.

The question remains: will elaborate pathways and trails alone promote cycling? The simple answer is no. Just being a "bike-friendly" city will also not work. Will political shame drive us away from cars and on to the bicycle? Not in droves.

Bike shop owners who have been around for more than one generation know the answer: take the kids out when they are young and have a lot of fun on bikes. When it's safe, let them ride to school. When they become teenagers, encourage them to get to school on a bike.

The trails will help. Having friends who also bike will help. Understanding something of the politics of reducing reliance on oil and reducing congestion will help. I believe one of the first and most important steps is the planning and construction of easy-to-use bike paths and lanes.

SEVEN

The Practice of Commuting

It is by riding a bicycle that you learn the contours of a country
best, since you have to sweat up the hills and coast down
them. Thus you remember them as they actually are, while
in a motor car only a high hill impresses you, and you have
no such accurate remembrance of country you have
driven through as you gain by riding a bicycle.

—ERNEST HEMINGWAY

Imagine a February morning in Seattle. It's dark until nine o'clock
or later. It's usually raining. The average temperature is under
forty degrees. Work starts at eight and the commute is twenty min-
utes by car, forty minutes by bus and forty-five minutes by bike.
The night before was fun, maybe a little too much fun. Make a deci-
sion. Ride the bike? Drive the car and pay for parking? Take the bus
and possibly sit next to the garlic capital of the world?

I commuted by bicycle every day for eight years. I averaged
more than five thousand miles a year just riding my bike to work.
Add to that my mileage on weekends, and I consistently rode more
than ten thousand miles a year. That's not a lot. I know several

cyclists who average twenty thousand miles a year and have been doing that distance for over twenty years. That's a bit of cycling!

Most people wonder why, and the only answer that comes to mind is that I still fit in the same size jeans I wore as a senior in high school. It's a vain reason, but usually the only one that works. During those years I also enjoyed a clear head, free of morning shock deejays, conservative anger, and the drone of NPR. I was more productive, having burned off nervous energy, and was ready to sit and get some work done.

My current employment is in an industrial complex that is not easily or safely accessible by bike. I also have a hectic schedule that will see me arrive very early or require me to stay very late. So, I no longer commute by bicycle for these reasons. My cycling now focuses on regular training rides either during the middle of the day or on weekends, as it did even when I commuted.

But also look at the math. Notwithstanding that some work centers more difficult to access than others, if I traveled five thousand miles in my car, and if gas costs more than three dollars a gallon and oil changes cost thirty dollars, I would save close to a thousand dollars a year or the cost of some really good steak, scotch, and desserts.

Most people I know who commute by bicycle are on the fringe of being cultists. Friendly and smart cultists, but cultists nonetheless. They are more fervent in their pursuit of cycling than some racers. Not many, but some.

> "In Tokyo, a bicycle is faster than a car for most trips of less than 50 minutes!"
> —www.strangefacts.com/facts1.html

BicyclingLife.com published a 1997 study conducted by Dr. William E. Moritz, Ph.D., of the University of Washington. The study was admittedly unfunded, and Dr. Moritz fully disclosed his intent to get as much information as he could with an unfunded survey. The results were interesting. Here is a sampling of the results:

- 81% of respondents who considered themselves bicycle commuters were male.

- The average age was thirty-nine.

- The average household income was greater than $45,000 a year.

- 58% considered themselves "professionals."

- 44% owned at least one car.

- 12% owned no cars.

- 69% of respondents were between twenty-five and thirty-nine years of age.

- Respondents commuted an average of 7.3 miles a day for an average of over three thousand miles a year.

- 57% indicated there were shower facilities at work.

- 39% said that weather would be the reason to stop bicycle commuting.

- 87% indicated they wore a helmet all of the time

- An average of $714 was spent by respondents each year commuting by bicycle, which included the cost of the bicycle.

I did not see in this survey any mention of how commuters dealt with the dress requirements of a professional career and commuting by bicycle. One man I work with trained for triathlons by commuting to work; he drove to work on Mondays to stock his office with shirts, slacks and shoes. He stuffed all of the soiled clothing into his pack on Friday and rode four days a week.

There are several types of bags that attach to the bicycle and are created specifically for the commuter. Designers have attempted to address the issue of professional clothing; some have succeeded and some have not. Many commuters do not need professional clothing and are not as concerned about wrinkles when they get to work

The most pressing issue for the commuter, and maybe especially for co-workers, is the availability of showers. A long, hard commute in the summer is going to have the desired effect: lots of sweat and hard work. Coworkers don't mind the hard work; it's the sweat they get fussy about!

Convincing a company to install showers might be a daunting task. You can find ideas to help make your case for corporate support on several websites, listed in Appendix Three. The reasons given for corporations to encourage this practice are fairly universal and are usually offered by municipalities whose vested interest is to reduce automobile commuting. Here area few of them:

Bicycles take up less space and certainly fewer parking spaces, potentially reducing the cost of employee parking.

Some municipalities contend corporations see a reduction in health-care costs. Cyclists are not sedentary, and in fact enjoy better than average fitness, thereby reducing need for medical care.

Several municipal sites referred to a study completed at UCLA that I was unable to verify, which claims cyclists are more alert and enjoy higher productivity than those commuting by car.

These sites also posit that corporations encouraging bicycle commuting are looked on favorably by prospective employees and the local community as well, thereby improving their public image.

These arguments are convincing to those who already believe in the benefits. Normally, corporations make the effort not so much to encourage bicycle commuting, but more so simply not to discourage the practice. They do not see the benefit of adding showers and office space designated specifically for bicycle storage. There is, however, strength in numbers.

The Sacramento Transportation Management Association contends that almost two percent of the commuting population in the four-county area around Sacramento commutes on bicycle, claimed to be the highest percentage in the nation. Second to Sacramento is Phoenix, with almost one and a half percent of the commuting population traveling by bicycle.

These percentages may not seem impressive, but they are considerably higher than the less than one percent quoted ten years ago. While these communities have succeeded in encouraging voluntary participation, consider the position taken by Seattle and the King County area.

In 1991, the Washington State Legislature passed a Commute Trip Reduction Law mandating that employees generate plans to encourage employees to seek out alternate modes of commuting to work. The law was directed primarily at companies with one hundred or more employees. These were considered major employers. The focus was very simple and straightforward: reduce the raw number of drive-alone commutes by subsidizing car pools, van pools, bus passes, and bicycle commuting by providing storage and even change/shower facilities. There was no set action plan required of any employer; companies just needed to meet some very aggressive numbers for reducing drive-alone commuting.

The Office Survival section of crazycolour.com links to Over Forty Reasons to Bike to Work. They cite the origin of this list as ibike.org. The highlights of this list are interesting. There are of course the obvious reasons. Often people do not have a driver's license and need to get to work anyway. Bicycle commuting saves money. It is easier to park a bike, and usually cheaper. Bicycle commuting reduces air and noise pollution. It reduces road wear.

They also cite some not-so-obvious reasons. You can dress funny, in colorful spandex, and get away with it. You can sweat like crazy, cleaning the pores, and not need a sauna. You will look better because of healthier skin and stronger muscle mass. The vain among us applaud this.

Finally, ibike.org claims that biking to work is therapeutic and beneficial to your mind, body, and spirit. I like this contention, but there is a caveat. Bicycling to work can be irritating, frustrating, and even dangerous.

Some people believe bicycles are for children to ride on the sidewalk on Sunday morning. The law in all the states sees bicycles as slow-moving vehicles, and allows them the first three feet of roadway inside the white line, not outside on shoulders that are inconsistent, littered with debris, and usually too narrow. This is where the conflict begins, especially for commuters.

Many cities, especially Seattle, have redesigned some streets, allowing for designated bicycle paths in an attempt to move cyclists from busy streets to designated areas free from automobiles. This is a double-edged sword. Engineers in the city of Bellevue, Washington, are adamant that cyclists belong only on these designated paths and not on any street that does not have such a path. While the plan allows for safer commutes for some, it begins to convince motorists that cyclists do not belong on the street, and they're eager to share that opinion with cyclists, usually using horn blasts, insults, and even broken bottles thrown in front of the bike.

How can this be beneficial to the Mind, Body and Spirit? I understand there are aggressive and unhappy people who take some strange pleasure in trying to cause me harm and at least strike fear in me. They exist everywhere, even when I ski or walk along the beach. My peace comes not from avoiding them entirely or confronting them, but from knowing their parameters. I pursue my peace and joy in spite of them.

When I used to commute by bicycle in Seattle, I went down Denny Way to 15th Ave NE, ending up in Ballard. It was the most obvious route to work, but over the sixty-plus weeks I made the commute, I was invariably involved in shouting matches and was even pushed into the blackberry bushes. One man in a pickup truck stopped and wanted to beat me up. I am not necessarily a pacifist when attacked, but I didn't provoke him and let the blustering bravado pass. He was late for work and a fight with me was going to make that problem even worse.

Driving back this same route one evening, a garbage disposal truck hit me with a security chain on the back and launched me over a car into the gravel on the side of the road. A fellow employee saw this incident and drove me home, and I soaked the road rash in the tub for several days.

I stuck with the commuting in spite of this. When my job location changed, I discovered the obvious: some routes are quieter than others and commuting *can* be beneficial to body, mind, and spirit. Map out routes that do not serve industrial areas serviced by large trucks. Try to avoid thoroughfares that are not bicycle-friendly. Usually these are heavily traveled streets with very frustrated drivers who will lash out at anything they perceive to be impeding their progress.

After my job location changed, my new route was through neighborhoods and along narrower but less-traveled streets. My commute was then normally without incident and really did contribute to my mental, physical, and spiritual health. To find an alternate route, first look for suggested bicycle routes on municipal websites. Failing this, stop by the local bike shops and ask. I suggest asking someone who is not into swerving through traffic to find the shortest route. Bicycle clubs typically have information about safe commuting and also discuss this topic at length during club meetings. It is worth joining a club and getting to know other bicycle commuters.

One legal assistant who works in downtown Seattle commutes from the top of Queen Anne Hill. There are several safe, quiet routes to and from work for him, but I challenged him to ride back up Queen Anne Avenue, known to Seattle natives as the Counter Balance, where the weights used to run under the street, pulling the old trolley car system up the steep hill. And it *is* steep. He worked at it over several weeks, usually dashing off to the side halfway up to find a flatter, easier way to the top. But finally he tackled the Counter Balance and, along with a handful of other bicycle commuters, tackles the hill every day. He has also met his target weight-loss goals over the past year. His commute is now more about accomplishments than it is saving a few bucks.

Establishing a goal to conquer a difficult route, and thereby becoming physically stronger, or simply losing ten or twenty excess pounds, are all the reasons many people need to commute. The result is usually a happier, healthier person, in spite of some of the caveats I listed above. One young man who joined the University of Washington cycling team on a lark suffered through the first year of training. He was dropped from the pack several times simply because he could not keep up. During the second year, he was aware of his increased strength, ability to sleep better at night, increased appetite, and ultimately his ability to keep up. He had no ambition of belonging to a professional racing team; he was most interested in forming like-minded friendships and attaining a level of physical conditioning he never thought was possible.

All of the sites referred to in this chapter consistently point to one final benefit of bicycle commuting, and one I have absolutely experienced: increased energy and a higher level of intellectual awareness. Although I cannot commute presently, but I find the time to ride outside of work for this very reason. I watch other employees slog to the coffee machine every morning after a frustrating drive and complain about how tired they are and how much work they have. I don't share that problem. At fifty, I have more energy than I should have. I have no problem taking on my work and the work not done by others, and so far I have the approval of my bosses and my longevity at work to prove that. The UCLA study quoted on one website would be useful if scientific evidence is necessary.

I know it is true and simply invite people to try it.

EIGHT

Finding Community on a Bike

There is nothing on this earth more prized
than true friendship.

—St. Thomas Aquinas

While there is an opportunity to join cycling communities to improve the bicycle commute, commuting is typically an individual pursuit, unless a large group of people lives and works in the same vicinity. The focus of this chapter is to explore opportunities for cyclists to share their experience with other devoted cyclists.

I have lived in a religious community, belonged to a gated community, joined several virtual communities, and participated in public hearings that help set community standards and the legislation required to support them. There is no debate really on the fact that we are anxious to join or create communities. There is generous debate on the inherent value of community.

I find virtual communities wanting. Myspace.com and similar virtual communities where one might think to find cycling partners or potential mates interested in cycling raise expectations that are rarely met. Getting there requires wading through a myriad of erotic photographs, thousands of groups with few real members, and a complete lack of any walk away value.

There are studies on the effect these virtual communities have on social skills. My own experience tells me it can be good—but it is usually bad. It might be necessary to consider why the community exists to determine if any value will come from joining. There is considerable press regarding the men (and a few women) who lurk in these virtual communities, attempting to make contact for sexual purposes with young teenagers and children. One virtual community was criticized for allowing prostitutes to advertise for free.

Other types of communities would not tolerate this activity. While there are predators looking for children in playgrounds and malls, small and large communities alike reject this activity and provide punishment for those who participate in it. One of the essential tasks of a social community then might be that of collective protection.

While living in a religious community, I discovered the purpose was to support each other in specific spiritual growth. It was easy to be a devout Catholic in the seminary because everyone else was, too, and there was no criticism for participating in daily devotions, criticism that might exist outside of that community.

Naked Cycling?

"The ride is primarily an activist event as you can see from the photos, www.dougdo.com/?p=7, where people have painted slogans on their bodies. The ride isn't really about riding naked, it's about promoting cycling as an environmentally sound form of transportation. By doing it naked, we get a lot more attention for the cause than we would otherwise. I also participate sometimes in the Critical Mass rides, but 1,000 clothed riders for Critical Mass get a lot less attention than 100 naked ones."

My experience with most cyclists is they are notoriously independent thinkers. I have met very few who are devout about any kind of religion. But clubs devoted to cycling abound and the numbers continue to grow. There are clubs for racing, touring, general fitness, and acquiring discount parts. There are clubs for single women, gay men, families, senior citizens. Some clubs are rigidly managed, others loosely knit, but both kinds survive. They each seem to fulfill a human need, the need to belong and find support.

The risk of extremely narrowly focused communities is the potential for not providing a sense of belonging or support to the members. When this happens, the community dies. The members begin to die spiritually.

Thriving communities offering the most to their members are intentional and offer a broad-based purpose. I have joined and left several bicycle clubs. I found elitist arrogance, bigotry, and excessive competition—it simply wasn't worth the membership dues. I am sure there are people who thrive in that environment, just as there are people who love to be picked to enter an exclusive club, leaving everyone else waiting outside, rejected. I do not. I joined a bicycle-racing club as an ad hoc member during two extended trips to Europe. It provided the best experience; these were local amateurs my own age who rode for the love of riding and sometimes would not even show up for the race. It was the friendship they wanted. I also joined a large urban club with several hundred members and found it alienating; I either rode in the pack, letting the alpha dogs tell me how to ride, or I rode alone. I saw no need to pay membership dues if I was going to ride alone.

Many people spend their lives in search of community: The right community, one that is nurturing and supportive. For some it can be found in something as simple as bicycle touring.

Bicycle touring is often perceived as dirty and difficult. This perception of bicycle touring is unfounded, especially given the four-star guided bicycle tours available. One might think the daily ride will always be in excess of one hundred miles, or all of the accommodations will in campgrounds with desperate shower facilities, cooking over a smoldering campfire. I happen to think that this is a good time, but most people want a bed, a shower, and a hot meal at a table.

A quick search on the Internet dispels the discomfort myth. I selected four countries, Peru, Slovenia, Wales, and Mongolia. I found several fully supported bicycles tours offered by companies centered either in the United States or in the respective country. The tours offer hotel or *pension* accommodations, meals, and mechanic support, and the average daily ride was about thirty-five miles. Some cyclists might find this to be a little wanting in distance, but they have their tours as well, offering them the opportunity to ride ahead of the *peleton* of the Tour de France in excess of one hundred miles a day with a finish-line view of the race.

The tour of Peru is sold as a moderately challenging mountain bike ride that offers mostly hotel accommodations, but also five nights of camping out of the total fourteen-day tour. The ride is fully supported and climbs through the Andes up to an altitude of thirteen thousand feet and offers a stop at Machu Pichu. The general description of the tour promises rigorous cycling for all levels, which usually means when you're done for the day you get in the truck and go to the next destination while the stronger cyclists press on the whole distance. They describe the nightlife as "wild," and I will leave it up to you to figure out what that means.

The tour through Slovenia is a seven-day ride through the Julian Alps. Slovenia is an independent country, once part of Yugoslavia. It is offered as a classic old European tour that is fully supported, starting with airport transfers and going right up to the nightly hotel and dinner. They make a point of informing their clients that they do not buy your booze, and if you want to visit the tourist spots the entrance fees are on you.

The Wales tour offers a seven-day tour of the Pembrokeshire Coast National Park, said to be the most beautiful coastline in all of Europe. They center the tour in a former priory and offer a bicycle-free day during which you can hike or even surf.

Finally, what appears to be among one of the most challenging offerings I found is a tour in Mongolia starting in Gobi and ending up in Lake Khovsgol, traversing the Khangi Mountains in central Mongolia. The accommodations are tents-only, except for the first night in Gobi and the last night in Lake Khovsgol. The ride is promised to be one hundred percent off-road following rough jeep tracks. Of the four, this one sounds most exciting to me.

A classmate at Naropa University took his second summer off and packed a bicycle on a plane. He carried virtually no luggage; just a medium-sized bag that hooked to his bicycle saddle. In this he carried some changes of essentials, spare cycling shorts, his passport, and money. He rode from Amsterdam to Barcelona by way of Berlin and Vienna. He ate in restaurants and stayed in youth hostels or cheap hotels. He averaged eighty miles a day and found he had time to see more than he ever anticipated. Because he ate so much along the way, he lost fat, but actually gained weight in muscle. He discovered how much easier it was to ride a bicycle through Europe, easier than even supposedly bicycle-friendly Boulder. Bicycle shops in small villages might have charged him for the spare tubes he needed, but always made sure he had a free meal from the kitchen upstairs.

The most rewarding aspect of the trip was the simplicity of pedaling a bicycle through a foreign country and the closeness he felt to the people and culture. He had traveled in Europe on previous vacations using rented cars and trains. He claims he experienced more on the bicycle in five weeks than he had in the accumulated months of previous European trips.

One might not think a bicycle tour with a couple of priests could be any fun. I was privileged, however, to be included in their tour of the San Juan Islands. Not only did they stay in schools and well-appointed houses belonging to the Church, all of which were fully equipped with food, showers, beds, and laundry for free, but they had access to phones, faxes, emails, and television. The most interesting part of the tour was arriving at Shaw Island and being assisted off the ferry by the nuns who operate the docking facility for the state of Washington. The priests knew the nuns, and of course we had another free place to stay. In the morning, I was invited to the celebration of the communal Eucharist in their basement chapel, which had a natural spring running through it. During the more quiet times of the mass, two frogs serenaded us.

Beyond the bicycle tour, there is community to be found in the collective commitment to the bicycle. Organizations in the Seattle area like the Cascade Bicycle Club and Critical Mass are two such examples. Members of both clubs, however, might object to being included in the same sentence as the other.

The Cascade Bicycle Club's website states that the "Cascade Bicycle Club is a non-profit organization creating more livable communities by promoting health and recreation through bicycle activities, advocacy and education."

The website hosted by someone associated with the Critical Mass rides in Seattle notes that "on the last Friday of every month, in over one hundred cities around the world, cyclists congregate to ride in demonstration and celebration. Critical Mass has no leaders or set agenda, and people come together to ride for many different reasons. Just a few of those reasons are . . . to assert cyclists' right to the road, to promote bikes as a fun, healthy viable alternative to cars, to build a greater sense of community, to get more folks on bikes, or simply to celebrate bike love and ride in solidarity with like-minded individuals and have some fun."

The Cascade Bicycle Club is a large organization serving the interest of mainstream cyclists. There are hundreds of such clubs around the country, sponsoring safety classes, local and long distance rides, and through the Cascade Bicycle Club Education Foundation reaches out to cyclists, motorists, and legislators to educate the local community on matters of interest to cyclists.

In Seattle, Critical Mass gathers in Westlake Center in downtown Seattle and rides the street *en masse,* often blocking intersections and slowing traffic on streets to a cyclist's pace. The event is well coordinated with the Seattle police, and they often escort the group—as well as issue citations for traffic violations committed by the cyclists. There has been a history of angry exchanges between cyclists and motorists and even recently with two King County deputies, but for the most part the rides are fun demonstrations intended to awaken the local community to the presence of cyclists.

In cycling, there is a community for everyone. The community one finds in touring is often focused on mutual exploration of new and exotic environments such as Mongolia. There is the shared hardship or the joy of a magnificent view.

Cyclists on tours depend mostly on the organizers if they have paid for a package, but if not, they depend on each other. The group is a small, isolated community that survives because of this agreement to assist each other. Unlike reality shows that pit one team of participants against the other and ultimately each other, this type of community is sustaining, supportive, and collaborative.

Ask to ride with the group before joining. If they ride too fast, look for a group that accommodates your speed. It is typically a good idea to find a group of people within some range of your own age. I've ridden with much younger racing teams, and they seemed uncomfortable with my age, even though I was more than able to keep up (and in fact drafted them through the headwinds). I was not going to try and force myself into their group. I have encountered the problem of riding with a group that I found to be way too slow for my normal rides, but enjoyed the company anyway.

People will migrate toward the community that gives them what they need, and cyclists are no exception. Some want the comfort of a large, diversified community that serves the needs of the mainstream cyclist and others want to feel they belong to a cutting-edge community dedicated to changing society. Community comforts us and when we find comfort, it doesn't matter about ideology or the style of bike they ride.

NINE

Riding Solo

Just as the ideal of classic Greek culture was the most perfect
harmony of mind and body, so a human and a bicycle
are the perfect synthesis of body and machine.

—RICHARD BALLANTINE

There is risk to riding alone. Two friends of mine know this all
too well. One was caught seventy miles from home in the
desert of California without a cell phone and two flat tires. He used
up his spare tube and canned air on the first flat. He walked for
three hours in ever-increasing heat before a vehicle stopped and
gave him a ride. Fortunately, he had enough water in his Camelbak
to survive.

The other gentleman rode his mountain bike out into some of the
most remote areas of Eastern Washington and fell, breaking his hip.
He also did not have a cell phone, and there was no one within
twenty miles of the accident.

Before I extol the virtues of riding alone, allow me to suggest a
bare-minimum list of supplies. I learned from years of mountain-
eering that everything on this list is important.

Get a cell phone, even if you decide not to use it as a primary phone. Bring two spare tubes and get enough cartridges of canned air to fill two or three flats and to top off your tires in case they somehow go low. Bring a supply of bandages. Bring more water than you think you will need, especially if you are riding into a remote area. I always need to change clothes, especially if I sweat and the air decides to go cold. I chill instantly and always bring dry jerseys and socks. In Washington State, there is a good chance there will be no rain from late June until late September, but outside of that, the rains can come on fast and cold. The first week of May this year promised to be a comfortable high sixties with mostly sunshine, but in fact on Saturday when I chose to ride the rain came in sheets and the temperature dropped into the forties. Even with arm-warmers, a rain jacket and extra gloves, I froze to the point my fingers and toes grew numb. I had prepared for a spring rain, and we got a late winter torrent instead! My stomach usually cannot take food while I am exercising, but I always have two or three energy or breakfast bars. I know that if I need to stop to let weather pass or handle a mechanical failure, I will bonk. Finally, carry some tools like Allen wrenches, screwdrivers, and box wrenches. The small tool sets sold by your local bike shop will have the most commonly needed tools.

Riding partners laugh at my stuffed hip bag until they need something from it—like water, food, or an air cartridge. But now it's time to ride alone.

My job requires that I have several intense technical or personal conversations every day, so I love riding alone with no one to talk to. The solitude does more than just help me process information; it allows me to regenerate the energy I need to engage in my work. I am familiar with many triathletes who might prefer to ride with a group, but their sport mandates that they cannot benefit from the draft of another competitor, so they train alone. Finally, I know a few people who are truly lone wolves who just don't like other people and do everything alone.

No matter where you fall in this spectrum, riding alone can be more rewarding than trying to find a group you are able to keep up with or that will ride at your pace . . . or with which you feel a good sense of community.

Riding with the right group provides me with the feeling of belonging to a community, as I discussed in the previous chapter. Riding alone offers a completely different opportunity. I am able to listen to myself. I have a habit of muttering about my anxiety under my breath, especially if I do not know its cause. If I am deeply concerned about something, I talk to myself silently, though my lips move.

I listen to my anger. I am able to say the angry words I want to say and see how they sound. I want to yell at my boss, and can do that pushing twenty-three miles an hour—and do it with some conviction, realizing that if I ever spoke the words to her face I would be fired. I get angry with my family and verbalize it in the most extreme forms cycling alone. When I return, I realize the energy behind that anger has been released, and I am able to deal with them more rationally.

I have solved complex problems with our computer systems while cycling alone. I see the code structures in my head after I verbally describe the problem. The solutions come to me cycling—and usually not at any other time. I am so busy in the hallways, talking to people, that I don't reflect well on the problem at my desk. It is only when I have hit a consistent cadence for a prolonged period that the solution develops in my mind. I have frequently called our network administrator from a ride and told him the solution—and it works.

I can listen to myself so closely I lose track of time and distance. I can sense progress in muscle development by comparing responses to similar strains from a previous ride. I know when I am going to get sick. I know when I am going to have problems at home.

I can also listen to others. I typically accept people at face value when I first meet them, but as their story unfolds I find the inconsistencies, and I can begin to piece together patterns. These ultimately may not bother me, or they may reveal a person I need to avoid, but I trust this process inherently.

I figured out who stole one of our projectors while riding alone and knew the person needed a cash infusion to pay off tuition the third week of every quarter. During the third week of the next quarter I watched him slide another projector, worth four thousand dollars, into his backpack. He was expelled from the school.

I know many people in very responsible positions, and they all agree they don't have time to think. That is precisely what cycling alone gives me. When I don't get much time for this, I begin to make mistakes, or tasks are not completed on time. I find myself trying to think through processes quickly and get workable, but impermanent, solutions.

I was required to sit in chapel in the seminary at five-thirty every morning for meditation. I usually slept until the bells in the tower adjacent to the church pealed out the beginning of mass. I am certain the fine monks I studied under are better at that than I am, and gain life-changing insights in their morning meditations. I am no good without a few cups of coffee first. I didn't understand the power of listening to myself, others, and the world around me on a bicycle until after I left the seminary and got back on my bike. Ultimately, my thinking while cycling led me to leave the seminary altogether and to find the focus of my life in academics and writing.

TEN

JLC for Your Bike

All bicycles weigh fifty pounds. A thirty-pound bicycle needs a
twenty-pound lock. A forty-pound bicycle needs a ten-pound
lock. A fifty-pound bicycle doesn't need a lock.

—AUTHOR UNKNOWN

As I began my exposure to the American version of Bud-
dhism at Naropa University, I overheard the story of a
young monk who was telling his master about all of the internal
anxiety and trouble he was experiencing. The master asked him if
he had washed his bowl and made his bed, and the young monk
indicated he had not. The master told him to go wash his bowl and
make his bed and the anxiety would go away.

I know this to be true, and I knew it before I was exposed to Bud-
dhism. Keep my life in order, and I lower my anxiety; allow my life
to fall apart, and I experience anxiety. If I don't pay my bills on
time, creditors call, and I am troubled. If I return tools I borrow, my
neighbors like me.

I took up bicycle mechanics as a way to save money and discov-
ered it was as valuable to me as riding itself. To be able to properly

repair something I hold so dear, and to pass that skill along to someone so they can continue to ride, is a prayer in itself.

I particularly like building and truing wheels. A wheel will stay true if each spoke is tightened to exactly the same tension. The physics are fairly easy to understand when you consider the forces at work. I have challenged old-school mechanics who claim they can achieve this perfection by feeling the spoke and "playing" them like guitar strings. The tensiometer I use to measure spoke tension usually catches them plus or minus five to ten pounds of tension on various spokes.

Building a wheel is slow, quiet, exacting work. I do not build them for commercial resale; there is no money in building a perfect wheel and taking two hours to do it. I would not want to pay for the time when a machine can take very good materials and produce a reasonably good wheel that I can then take home, loosen without completely disassembling, and rebuild to perfection.

Later in this book I'll discuss what is necessary to become a mechanic and perhaps even own a bike shop. This is a step taken by those who have fallen even more deeply, some say foolishly, in love with cycling. My intent here is to make sure you are enough aware of what is necessary to keep your bike in optimum condition to do some of the work yourself—or at least be able to talk intelligently with your mechanic and get the work you need.

The occasional cyclist may never use his or her bicycle enough to need a tune-up or an overhaul. If you ride more than a few hundred miles a year, you definitely need tune-ups and eventually an overhaul. Sealed bearings go bad. Bottom brackets fill with water and mud, wear the parts down, and even loosen. Wheels hit ruts and rocks and go out of true. Personal safety is at risk if a bicycle is not properly maintained.

It is easy to fix a bicycle correctly. There is rarely a bicycle that cannot be repaired. Even when my brother-in-law backed his truck over his mountain bike, all I needed was a cheap surplus frame. I painted it and simply moved the parts from the fractured frame to the new one. Within a day the bike was completely safe and operational.

The key, however, is knowing how to do it correctly. I attended a bicycle mechanics school and learned how to properly assemble and repair any bicycle. One of my fellow students was then a chief helicopter mechanic. He had spent the better part of ten years in school learning and re-learning everything possible about all of the military helicopters for which he was responsible. The objective for him was always the same: safe flights that returned soldiers after a mission. The helicopter had to start, fly, shoot, return, and land every time. He decided to take the course in bicycle mechanics because he found most shops he visited did not have the same mindset, so he was determined to do it correctly himself.

Tune-ups are often priced very cheaply because it usually means up-selling parts and components that are highly overpriced. I often suspect this when I see a sign offering a tune-up for nineteen ninety-five, but with none of the actual services actually listed. There are a few shops that will list, in detail, what a tune-up will include. Some shop owners will automatically require replacement of brake pads and a complete security check as part of the package. If the services are not listed, ask. If a clear list of the services is still not offered, go to a different shop.

One young mechanic in Seattle was told by a shop owner how to perform tune-ups: oil the chain, check for brake grip and adjust as necessary, make sure the shifting is fairly accurate, and wipe the bike clean. He was allowed a total of fifteen minutes on each tune-up, and in spite of the assurance of the owner to the customer that every bike was ridden for a safety test, the mechanic was rarely allowed to do this.

On the following pages is a guide to what you should expect in a seasonal tune-up.

Tune-Ups

1. Conduct a brief safety check with the customer present and note any serious aberrations. Note condition of tires, chain, and brake pads.

2. Test-ride the bicycle and determine the level of functionality of all the components.

3. Systematically note the condition of shifting, braking, steering, and pedaling, and note any sounds that might indicate potential failure in headsets, bottom brackets, and hubs.

4. Once the bike is on the rack, note how true the wheels are. A good mechanic will also check front and rear hubs for proper adjustment.

5. Properly adjust the shifting and braking, then tighten all connections to their proper torque value. Tires are inflated to the proper level.

Good mechanics will note any serious issues on the work ticket for the customer's information.

The bike should be thoroughly cleaned, the chain and cables properly oiled. The mechanic takes the bike out for a ride and shifts into every gear and brakes, and then the bike is wiped down thoroughly, leaving it clean and ready to ride,

Be wary of the shop that doesn't make this effort to inform you of the condition of all crucial parts of your bike. They may not know how to complete this level of tune-up. Ask your mechanic what he or she intends to do before you leave it for the tune-up.

The Overhaul

The overhaul should be just that, a complete overhaul. When I charged one hundred and twenty-five dollars for an overhaul, this is what my customers got:

Inspection with Customer Present

1. Mark seat post and stem where customer has them set.

2. Check chain line and frame alignment.

3. Test shifting and braking.

4. Check chain wear. (There is a specific tool for this. Ask your mechanic if he or she has one.)

5. Test any play in head and bottom bracket.

6. Check for wheel true and any play in hubs. Remove front wheel and using drop out alignment tools, check for fork true.

7. Ask the customer if there are any specific performance issues.

8. Tell the customer of any serious safety or performance issues.

The Overhaul

The mechanic should systematically and completely disassemble the bike.

Take a minute to look around the shop area, without violating the shop's policy on not allowing customers in the mechanics' area. If it is disorganized and dirty, you can almost bet there will be no systematic approach to anything.

In a complete overhaul, the mechanic will remove all cables because they will be replaced unless the customer has specified not to do that.

The headset has been inspected, but not yet overhauled. The lock nut, stem, and fork are carefully removed, and the top and bottom races are carefully inspected. The bearings are inspected. All items are properly cleaned with solvent and dried.

The bottom bracket should be completely disassembled. If there are sealed bearings, they are inspected for wear. Loose bearings and the cap faces are inspected for wear. The spindle is inspected for wear and whether it has been bent over the years. All parts are properly cleaned with solvent and dried.

Frame and fork alignment techniques will vary according to the materials used. It is easy to correct alignment on a steel frame and fork. Other materials, such as carbon fiber and titanium will not typically have an issue and so many mechanics will skip this step. During the inspection, the customer should note any serious deficiencies in balance and steering that might indicate improper alignment.

Reassembly of headset and bottom bracket: If the cups on the headset need to be replaced, a properly sized cup will need to be pressed into place. A good mechanic will check spindle protrusion on the bottom bracket during reassembly. The mechanic will use something like a lithium-based grease known for its water-repellent effects. The headset and bottom bracket are properly reassembled. Mechanics have their own test as to whether the bearings are too tight or too loose. Some refer to this as a "hint of play" in both bearing assemblies. The bottom line is the correct adjustment so the bearings do not wear out prematurely or the assembly does not fall apart.

Front and back wheels true: Check for true and consistent spoke tensioning. A wheel may appear to be true, but the spoke tensioning may differ widely between spokes. The wheel will soon go out of true. Some mechanics are excellent at finding this, others have no clue. "Play" your spokes gently like playing a harpsichord and you will feel immediately if the spokes are all set to the same tension or if some are too tight and others loose. If this condition exists, a complete overhaul would include properly adjusting the spokes so that all spokes are tensioned the same. I use a tensiometer; ask your mechanic if he or she uses one in an overhaul.

Front and back hubs: It is generally not necessary to remove and gear cassettes unless there is a problem with the back spinning.

Typically the mechanic will only need to inspect sealed bearings. With loose bearings, the mechanic should clean cones and bearings with solvent and repack them using the same "hint of play" adjustment to be certain the hubs are tightened correctly.

Brakes should be disassembled and cleaned. Pads should be replaced if there is visible sign of wear. I always included new pads in the price of the overhaul.

Derailleur inspection: I always removed the rear derailleur from the drop out and inspected how straight the drop out was in reference to the frame, using a drop out alignment bar. Ask your mechanic if he or she does the same. It is a quick and simple procedure and ensures that your derailleur sits in proper alignment with the frame and gears. The derailleur should be thoroughly cleaned and the small wheels oiled. The front derailleur usually needs cleaning, inspection for wear, and adjustment as part of a complete overhaul.

The final inspection should entail a head-to-toe test of the proper torque values of all adjustable nuts, bolts, screws, and hex nuts. Ask your mechanic if he or she knows about this and refer him or her to Sutherlands or a similar industry standard manual for these values. This inspection should also include a test ride and a final wipe-down. After a complete overhaul, the bike should be clean and fully functional.

The tune-up and the overhaul are best completed by qualified mechanics. The shop will carry liability insurance, and if the mechanic makes a mistake, the insurance will kick in. Cyclists who take on bearing repacks, head set adjustments, bottom bracket replacements, and similar tasks are typically not covered by insurance for their mistakes. If they adjust the stem higher than recommended, they risk breaking the stem off and falling face down on the bike and then the ground.

On a longer endurance ride, I witnessed a young woman (whose husband had adjusted her bottom bracket) career off the side of the road when her left crank fell off, causing her to lose control of the bike on a downhill section. I train on the Velodrome in Redmond, Washington, and witnessed a cyclist lose a right pedal as he sprinted around the southern bank. Fortunately, it was not in the middle of a scratch race and the other cyclists were far enough back to stop as he toppled over the handlebars and slid down the cement.

Consider the value of a properly adjusted bicycle. Also, take the time to become familiar with basic cleaning and adjustments that must be made before taking to the road. Qualified mechanics know the proper adjustments and torque values for all connections. Cyclists should know how to check if a pedal is tightened before they wheel it onto the track. Being familiar with proper cleaning and oiling of essential parts will minimize breakdowns. Learn how to change a flat and always carry a spare tube, pump, or air cartridge and levers.

Returning to the story of the monk who was feeling anxious, rather than telling him to go wash his bowl, I might suggest he clean his bike. As a mechanic, I was allowed to start charging a ten-dollar bike-cleaning fee, especially for the weekend mud warriors who could not take even five minutes to hose the bike down before dropping it off Monday morning to get a flat fixed. Water does not hurt a bike. If proper care is taken to oil the chain, cable housing ends, spoke nipples, and bearings that are not sealed in grease, there is nothing wrong with taking the bike through a high pressure car wash and getting it clean. When I see well-used bikes that are spotlessly cleaned, I sense a pride of ownership.

ELEVEN

The Ultimate Cycling Love Affair — Racing

> Don't buy upgrades;
> ride up grades.
> —EDDY MERCKX

*P*art of celebrating the human experience is becoming aware of the thrill of healthy competition. Competition sharpens the mind and typically brings out the best in anyone; tracking the progress of amateur to professional athletes can inspire and motivate toward increased activity and better health. As cyclists increase their participation in this sport, there is usually an increased awareness of and interest in organized competition.

There is a dark side of organized athletics, where soccer hooligans riot at the slightest provocation, where professional baseball players strike over making millions instead of mega-millions, and professional cyclists use banned designer drugs for enhanced performance. As bad as it seems to have gotten, however, the joy of watching pure competition always remains an important part of enjoying the complete cycling experience.

When it is pure, there are few sports as exciting to observe as cycling in all its manifestations. The objective typically is to use human strength to ride a bike across a specified distance faster than anyone else. In road cycling, this is achieved through races such as time trials, criteriums, longer road races, and, during the off-season, cyclo-cross, which follows a trail that is a mixture of cement, grass, trail, and mud.

Mountain bike racing includes single-track descents or extremely rough terrain, cross-country trail races, and trick expositions taking the mountain bike down stairs and over fences and tables.

BMX racing usually is focused on dirt tracks covered with various obstacles like jumps, soft dirt, and rough, undulating track. The use of wooden ramps in competition allows BMX enthusiasts to watch aerial tricks scored for risk and creativity.

Oval track racing has several types of races, some specific to wooden tracks and others to cement tracks. The excitement is enhanced by the fixed gear and the lack of any sort of brakes.

When Lance Armstrong reappeared in professional racing after fighting cancer, there was renewed interest in the Tour de France. As Armstrong began to win, he was interviewed more, and what struck my friends who had not been around bicycle racing was that he (and most everyone else racing at that level) was not very big. They were used to watching athletes in baseball, basketball, and football, where girth is usually beneficial. It would be extremely difficult for a three-hundred-fifty-pound lineman to ride a racing bike over a mountain pass and to beat out someone weighing almost a third of that. In bicycle racing, size matters.

Mountain and track racing usually include people of all sizes, as they require different strength and skill-sets for success. I know very few adult BMX racers; it's usually the province of children and teenagers, with the exception of aerial competitions where grown adults make a lot of money flying through the air on a bike.

It is said that the secret of life is simple: if you think about something, you become it. That happens to cyclists who begin to track bicycle racing. I know a sixteen-year-old young man who came in second in the Junior Nationals. I asked him why he races, and he immediately responded he could not imagine life without it.

My own foray into racing was not quite as focused, but I admit I loved the competition. Many events took place that prevented me from pursuing racing seriously, and I take responsibility for all of those events. I have always held that racing is the pinnacle of the love affair with cycling. It is the ultimate commitment.

I believe now that anyone can create the opportunity to pursue anything if they truly want it and that could have happened for me. I did not create the opportunity to compete at a professional level. I created other opportunities, perhaps for the better, perhaps not. I know I could now race at the master's level and, considering my condition, I could do well enough to satisfy this itch. It *is* an itch, a question, a perennial "what if."

I have created the life I want: I teach, read, lead other faculty members through their professional development, write, and ride. I believe I will add to that this year and actually enter some master's level cyclo-crosses. I'm choosing not to race on the track as my eyes are not as good as they were and the possibility of causing an accident is higher there. The simple fact is I always have new choices, and cycling has been how I take the time to think about my choices and always have the good health to enjoy them.

Part of that is to appreciate and celebrate the success of racers who pursue, and succeed at, the ultimate cycling commitment. No doubt I enjoy a leisurely ride with like-minded individuals, but there is nothing like watching the chase. I am able to follow all levels of racing, from junior nationals to the most elite professionals, thanks to the Internet and websites like cycling.tv and cyclingnews. com. The level of detail provided by archived video and even real-time Internet TV coverage, as well as the live written updates of races, keeps me more informed than ever on the sport. These advances in Internet-based reporting have enabled me to awaken more fully my appreciation of clean competition.

I enjoy the moment when someone crosses from being a spectator to being a competitor. When I train on the Group Health Velodrome in Marymoor Park in Redmond, Washington, I anticipate with mixed feelings the days when families take their slow mountain bikes on the track and start riding erratically around me and others, not considering—probably not even knowing—that our track bikes have only positive forward motion and no brakes!

The bright side to that is it might be a transition for someone from being on the sidelines to being on the track under the lights, but there has to be a learning curve there as well.

The easiest place for children to start racing is with the local BMX club. Any shop that is seriously into the BMX business will know the local clubs. BMX at the six-to-fourteen-year-old range is a family event and usually held in the early evenings. Older BMX racers get more serious and start traveling the circuit and, if they are good enough, often earning lucrative sponsorships in their midteens. I watched an MTV program showcasing an elaborate home belonging to a very young man. He'd earned the money racing BMX and endorsing products.

A website devoted to junior BMX racing in Western Australia indicates how widespread this form of bicycle racing has become. They define BMX as Bicycle Moto Cross, the pedal-powered version of the real thing. The typical BMX track is three hundred to four hundred meters in length and includes any number of jumps and turns of varying challenges.

BMX is also the most cost effective racing program for any child to participate in. They can use any sixteen-inch, twenty-inch, twenty-four-inch, and twenty-six-inch wheel diameter bike and inexpensively modify it for local competition. The more important modifications include padding on the handlebars and frames, as well as removal of any protruding devices such as bells, horns, etc.

As in most junior races, these clubs require face helmets, gloves, long-sleeved shirts, long pants, and covered shoes. Most clubs will loan or rent the essential helmets for the season if the participant cannot afford to buy one.

Starting out in off-road or mountain-bike racing is just as easy. Teambigbear.com, a website devoted to mountain bike racing in the Big Bear region of California, claims to offer "everything you always wanted to know . . . about racing your mountain bike." The site is fairly comprehensive and includes information on the types of mountain bike racing and the points system leading to the awards. A NORBA license is required.

NORBA stands for the National Off Road Bicycle Association, which was founded in 1983 to nurture a fledgling sport and recreational activity. In 1989, USA Cycling purchased NORBA and now represents their interests to the International Federation.

The most notable types of mountain-bike racing are the downhill time trial and the cross-country. The downhill is the most popular, as it requires racers to descend very steep terrain over rocks, logs, mud, and bushes. Racers wear full-face helmets, padded pants and shirts, and have no fear of hurtling head first over the handlebars when their fast-moving bike hits an immovable object.

Cross-country racing covers a variety of terrain, including some of the downhill, but primarily the rolling terrain of the local race. This type of racing is similar to a road race, with the exception that very little (if any) of the course is paved. The races are timed, but usually the first person to cross the finish line wins.

Track racing is a sport of esoteric appeal: the bike has one gear and no brakes, and the only way to stop is to slow down the pedaling motion. Stop pedaling and, legend has it, you fly off the bike.

That is not quite true and maybe those who bust urban myths might be interested in investigating.

There is nothing like the grit of a wooden or cement track that is between two hundred and four hundred meters long. The oval ends are banked and used for tactics. Most novices get up enough speed to do fine in what is referred to as the blue line, but become excessively nervous as they climb the steep oval bank going five miles an hour. The thought of tipping over is ever-present in their minds. Junior track racers are properly taught to maintain speed, ride in a straight line unless passing safely, and to use the banks for tactics and not for recreation.

There are various types of track races. Most notably is the American invention of the Madison, sometimes referred to as the Six Day Race. Named after the Madison Square Gardens, the race pits teams of two to seven riders against each other in a continuous race, lasting sometimes six days (hence the name). The team that rides the most laps in the allotted time wins. Some riders can cover forty to fifty laps, while others can ride twenty at a very fast pace. As riders fade, they signal their bench to get the next racer ready, and they are often pulled into the race by the fading racer (who might have a special handle sewn into their shorts).

The Keirin is a race led by a motorcycle; cyclists are allowed to draft behind the motorcycle—if they can. The Japanese invented the race, and it is fraught with jostling and elbowing to get behind the motorcycle until it peels off and the cyclists are left to race out the final laps.

The most popular track races are the scratch and pursuit. Scratch races usually comprise a determined number of laps; the racers all start together. They race the ten, twenty, or forty laps, and the winner is the first across the line. Teams often plant riders to block or slow down other major racers so the designated star can win more easily. In pursuit races, teams of one, two, or three racers start opposite from each other on the track and race until the other team is lapped or they cover the designated number of laps in the fastest time.

Track racing can be a little more difficult to enter, especially as a teenager. The track bike is specific to the track with its fixed gear and lack of brakes. Bicycle messengers with too much bravado ride them up and down city streets with impunity, but short of this, there's no other use for them. A good used track bike can cost five hundred dollars, whereas a new high-end bike for track racing can reach three and four thousand dollars.

The Group Health Velodrome, the outdoor bicycle-racing track near Seattle, offers Saturday training programs for adults and weekday programs for youth; track bikes can be borrowed for the training and then the racing events. Not many shops even sell track bikes, let alone loan them to aspiring racers.

Unlike BMX and mountain racing, track is a brute-force event with complex tactics, rather than a tactical race where winners depend on gravity or style to win. Road racers can often transfer their skill and desire to win across to track, but the best track racers are those who can drive the split-second shift in tactics as well as the relentless tempo of a pursuit or scratch race.

Finally, road racing has long been considered the grandfather of all bicycle racing. Dating back more than one hundred years now, the Tour de France pits cyclists against each other in a race that often covers more than two thousand miles in three weeks. With the exception of two breaks (for World War One and World War Two), the Tour de France has been going on since 1904. This race is still considered the most prestigious and draws the best talent road racing has to offer.

It was often believed in my lifetime that Americans were not good enough to race against Europeans and win. The problem was that, until Greg Lemond won, American cyclists were never considered serious contenders. The reality is that they were never given the opportunity to seriously try, which required membership in the exclusive boys' club of European cycling. In the past twenty-one years, Americans have won eleven yellow jerseys on the Tour. There are a few other notables, such as Andy Hampsten, winner of the Giro d'Italia in 1988; Bobbie Julich, who finished third in the 1999 Tour de France; Frankie Andreieu, who competed in several Tours; and Bob Roll, who has become famous commenting on Tours.

These racers came up through junior and U23 programs, allowing them to hone skills among a wide variety of competitors; they finally found themselves participating—if not being entirely welcomed—in European cycling. And now they're winning.

There is no mystery to this. There is a very vibrant and viable racing program for all ages in this country. There is no shortage of participants, thanks to the fame and example of all three American winners of the Tour de France.

Programs such as the Western Colorado Cycling Club Junior Development Program focus on introducing competitive cycling to children thirteen and older. This particular program developed what they refer to as a progressively tiered junior racing program, which also provides professional coaching and support. They provide physical and physiological preparation, training in competition behaviors, emotional and social behaviors, technical skills, tactical skills, and equipment knowledge.

In 1972, when I first owned a race quality bicycle, there was no local training program for children and teenagers. I was on my own, basically, to fantasize. This has changed. Every major city has a program similar to the Western Colorado Cycling Club program.

The Boat Street Criterium, held every April in Seattle, is a showcase not only of the collegiate racing programs, as well as the Cat Two, Cat One and Pro racers of the area, but of the junior programs as well. It is a short, easy course with mild hills and corners, designed to draw early-season racers. A criterium is usually held

"Today, there are approximately 215 NCCA (National Collegiate Cycling Association) member collegiate cycling clubs with over 2,500 member athletes. Each club belongs to a particular collegiate cycling conference, which is designated on the basis of the school's location."

—www.usacycling.org/news/user/story.php?id=261

on a smaller, well-marked circular course that challenges the racers' cornering, sprinting, and tactical skills. It is a fast-paced race made interesting by maintaining speed over numerous laps. During the race, racers can sprint for prizes on individual premium laps marked by an announcement and a cowbell.

Road races are longer events covering a larger route or end-to-end destination. These races cover anything from fifteen kilometers for juniors to the two-hundred-plus kilometer stage races in the Tour de France. Individuals can often enter alone or as a team, and it is up to the team and/or the coach to decide how well the team will work together to produce a single winner. Often collegiate racers are out for themselves and, in spite of the fact they have several teammates in the race, attempt to win it all alone. The better teams decide on tactics ahead of time and can thereby produce multiple levels of winners.

There are combinations of a criterium and road race that are often called a circuit race. Collegiate racing clubs are most familiar with the weekend omniums where there is usually a longer road race on Saturday, Sunday morning an individual or team time trial, and then Sunday afternoon various categories of the street criterium. It is common for collegiate races to begin early in the morning, followed by junior categories, and then finally the adult Three, Two, One and Pro categories to finish the day.

Some racers will use one bike for everything except track, and as they become more serious, buy race-specific bikes, as noted in chapter one. A common misconception among cyclists is the level of fitness and commitment necessary to race. Even at my age, I would be welcome, if not highly competitive, in many master's level races. The other competitors might be relieved to see me there, feeling quite good about lapping me in a crit or a down-and-dirty cyclo-cross race.

Some amateur Cat Two and One racers get caught up in the competitive spirit so much that they cross over from participating because it is fun to making a commitment to win consistently and be known for it.

Some cross over *beyond* a heartfelt commitment, and with the aid of performance-enhancing drugs, dial up the intensity in order to win simply for the sake of winning. The payoff can be good for clean and drug-enhanced racers both. Pro cycling contracts in the United States are modest, but once a racer has been accepted into a foreign team, typically somewhere in Europe, the money becomes real. Real enough to attract the cheaters. As I follow the collegiate and local amateur circuit, I hear rumors of some particularly good cyclists being accused of doping.

Most cyclists who cross from the amateur to professional ranks, however, are committed to clean racing. The challenge of winning through training, proper diet, tactics, and sheer grit over those who would enhance their performance with banned substances is worth the effort.

I know many people who choose to raise their children in homes that do not promote competitiveness. I come from just such a home and the valuable lesson taught to me is sometimes it is simply better to get along and share. I found as a teenager and adult competing in soccer, skiing, and cycling that my upbringing did not dampen what I consider to be a natural competitive nature in human beings; it helped focus my energies on competition that was healthy.

Instead of fighting and kicking for a soccer ball, I was able to focus on skills and became very good at ball handling, running, and scoring. I could help my team win without reverting to intimidation or violence. In bicycle racing, I could learn something from cyclists more committed to training when I witnessed their performance on a hill or in a sprint. Competition was not an end, it was a means to the end of refining and shaping athletic skills.

Other childhood friends who became aggressively competitive might have more money than I do, but I think I have a greater sense of internal peace and accomplishment. I will retire comfortably, but also happy and satisfied with my life. And, when I do retire, I have my health. During the physical after my fiftieth birthday, my doctor commented on my level of fitness; she noted it was much higher than even that of the typical twenty-something. I truly believe you pick your own life and, having picked cycling, I think the results have been better for me than an aggressive pursuit of money at all costs.

TWELVE

The Plunge from the Basement to Your Storefront

> I get to play golf for a living.
> What more could you ask for—
> getting paid for doing what you love.
> —TIGER WOODS

I once owned six bicycles at one time and was told I officially had a disease and it was time for me to either open a shop or get rid of some bikes. Many cycling enthusiasts take this very path, some to magnificent success and some to bankruptcy. The commitment to cycling at this point goes beyond recreation and fitness. At this point, cycling becomes a way of life, even a vocation.

I noted earlier in this book my brief foray into the bicycle business. Fred and Ruth Karacas left me in charge while Fred took a job flying planes over forest fires. My experience was delightful; I was not ultimately responsible and could therefore enjoy the day. I became more motivated to sell and enjoyed that process. I like working with people. The more I sold, the more money Ruth had to pay the bills. I realized early on that trying to squeeze a profit out of the bike business is not an easy road to retirement.

It is possible, though. Throughout my life, however, people have warned me not to work in my hobby. I can understand that, but cycling is more than a hobby for most shop owners: it is their life, and they could no more be a computer programmer than I could be a repo man. They need to be in a bike shop.

A successful path might look like this: An individual who really knows bikes well chances on a growing urban or suburban community that is being served minimally by a family-owned shop. He locates storefront space in an area frequented by all types of cyclists, and does his due diligence upfront and researches the local demographics, racing scene, commuter needs, and tendencies toward fitness. Once this is done, he begins to see what wholesalers will sell to him and at what price. Will the demographics support custom titanium bikes selling for thousands, or do the locals want basic commuter bikes like they use at the shipyards in Bremerton? (Shipyard workers have to walk more than a mile often to get to their workstations and an inexpensive commuter bike fills the bill. Olympic Bikes in Port Orchard sells and services a lot of them. The doctors, lawyers, and other well-paid professionals go to Ty Cycles in Seattle and eagerly order up the other end of the spectrum.)

Here is a list of considerations when thinking about owning a bike shop:

1. Is there enough money available to live on for six to twelve months?

> "In the year 2000, world bicycle production climbed to 101 million, more than double the 41 million cars produced. Sales of bikes are soaring because they provide affordable mobility for billions of people, increase physical fitness, alleviate traffic congestion, and do not pollute the air or emit climate-disrupting carbon dioxide."
>
> —*www.earth-policy.org/Updates/Update13.htm*

2. Is the bicycle shop just an attempt to be my own boss? (This is a very good motivation, but should not be the only one.)

3. Do I know the customer base in the area I want the shop?

4. Could I run the repair shop well when I cannot afford a mechanic?

5. Am I willing to work seven days a week until I can afford to sit in the office? (This might take several years)

6. Am I willing to go weeks at a time without riding a bike? (This happens a lot)

7. Do I understand concepts such as supply chain, floor financing, keystone . . . and other terms used in the business?

> Keystone is the profit margin usually applied to bicycles and accessories. It means the shop owner adds 100 percent of the wholesale price, and this determines the high end retail price. Obviously the shop owner will ultimately sell for market price.

The people who become the most successful apply standard business practices to the shop and do not treat it like a hobby. It would break their hearts to see the shop fail, and therefore they do not give bikes away to their friends. It is not a conduit for getting deals for family and friends. For the shop to be a success, they need to sell and make a profit.

It helps to love cycling beyond even being passionate about it. Successful shop owners are obsessed with cycling, and they pass this obsession on to their employees and customers. Not only have they opened their hearts to cycling, their hearts would stop beating *without* cycling.

Product lines are important inasmuch as they are a response to consumer demands in the neighborhood. A small logging community, for example, should not be categorized as a low-end product line. I have seen some very expensive full-suspension mountain bikes strapped on the back of logging trucks, and I see the connection; the truck drivers are often out in terrain not easily accessed by the routine mountain biker and the opportunity to dash down some of the most difficult single tracks imaginable is something they can access every day on the job. One small bike shop on the Olympic Peninsula saw this too, and sells race-quality full-suspension bikes where one might think there was no market for it.

One shop owner I know married into money, and his wife allowed him to stock a bike shop that might not work under normal circumstances. He has been able to turn this boutique shop into a regional mecca, carrying product lines and parts other shops would not be able to afford. Customers can go to one location and compare similar higher-end brands in one shop. The other draw he has is owning one of the northwest's largest collection of classic and collector bikes.

Someone can create a different path to success in the bicycle business by nurturing a devotion to cycling and earning a business degree. There are several national and regional chains of bicycle stores that are operated by efficient corporations. They have a product mix determined by careful study of demographics, and they sell at a discount because the wholesalers sell in bulk and commission their own line of products.

Beyond "wrenching" for a national or regional chain, there are always management opportunities at the store level as well as in the corporate office. I watched one friend rise from being a grease-covered "wrench" into a position where he is the senior buyer of bicycles for a very profitable regional chain, and he rides every day. If he'd pursued a career in law or insurance, he would not be happy. Instead, he makes a professional salary and surrounds himself with the love of his life—bicycles.

National bicycling magazines and bicycle trade magazines often carry advertisements selling bicycle shops. It can mean a great opportunity, but it can also mean the owner is dumping the store. I passed on a store in Colorado that simply wanted the prospective buyer to take over the lease and buy, at wholesale, existing stock. My credit has always been reasonably good, and I could have negotiated a fairly good deal with a national distributor. I made a mild attempt at conducting a due diligence and, rather than really go through the books, I passed. The eventual buyers have done well with the shop and have grown with their community. They added a line of BMX, resurrected the road-bike trade in the area and maintain a high profile in the mountain-bike trade. They added a line of skis and snowboards for sale as well as for rent. The shop is thriving and they seem to be living their dream—and are definitely living by their hearts.

The idea of owning a legitimate shop and applying the standard business practices I noted earlier in this chapter is a great path to follow. A few cycling enthusiasts think it is also a good way to enjoy super discounts on their favorite high-end components and bicycles. I've known a few to collectively form an s-corporation and seek out a relationship with a national or regional distributor to enjoy the often fifty to sixty percent price break a shop will charge for the same items. Fortunately for the legitimate shop owners, most distributors know this scam exists and require several things from the "shop owner" before they can establish a business relationship.

Seattle Bicycle Supply has a website serving shops in the Pacific Northwest Region. Before you can do business with them, the shop owner needs to complete the business application. It is for the most part a standard business application for a line of credit with the expected requests for bank information and credit references, but two required items typically separate the scam artists from legitimate shop owners. First, they require information about liability insurance specific to the retail bicycle industry. Second, they require a photograph of the front of the shop with signage in place. In short, if it is a legitimate shop, show them.

The bicycle shop owners I have known really do love bicycles and make a total life commitment to them. It is often a more difficult commitment, considering the notion I touched on earlier; it is often very difficult to make a living at your hobby. If cycling is a hobby, don't own a shop. That is the advice that resonates from every successful shop owner I have ever spoken with. When this commitment comes from the heart, then the seven-day weeks and the months without profit can be tolerated.

That is, until one day it all simply becomes too much. Some owners will never worry and rarely work more than two or three days a week. That breed is a rare one and their shops have usually been established for decades, if not for generations. The national chains can subsidize stores until they are established. But some owners will decide enough is enough and go back to work that sustains them properly.

There is something to consider here. I am always looking for a deal. I would like to pay wholesale for everything. I also understand the need to have the local shop. Where I live in Bothell, Washington, we have a very good local shop that has survived and has become established. It is close to my home and when I need tubes, air cartridges, a new saddle or even a whole bike, it is there and I am often willing to pay something more than I would at the large national chains to make certain the shop will be there. Of course, I have my limits, and would move on to the next shop the second I felt I got a bad deal. They have always been fair and honest with me, though, and I continue to buy some if not all of my parts and accessories from them.

When I was touring at the age of fifteen, my Puch Bergmeister broke down in the small town of Snohomish, Washington. I needed a front derailleur. The local hardware store in town had two Columbia single speeds and a few parts like horns and handlebar bells. A customer in the hardware store told me of an old guy from Europe who had a shop in his barn just outside of town. We walked the bikes the two miles to the barn and found a fully stocked shop with the exact derailleur I needed. His support came from the cyclists who rode out to Snohomish from Seattle and always stopped to buy one or two small things in hopes he would always be there when they needed him.

While completing a consulting commitment in Rochester, New York, I noticed an advertisement in a national bicycling magazine for a frame-building business. I made arrangements to visit the shop. The owner had been a Category One racer with professional ambitions, and abruptly decided to apply his metallurgy background and education to the art of frame building. His shop was equipped to build steel frames exclusively. The fabrication process was very efficient, so much so that one person could take raw stock and easily walk through the production line to a completed frame designed to a unique specification in two days, minus the painting. He told me that at the peak of production, he employed five frame builders, two of whom he had recruited from Europe.

Industries shift, and aluminum, carbon fiber, and even titanium frames became more popular than the heavy rigid steel frames. This particular business declined to the point where he was working outside the shop and building one or two frames a month. I passed on the opportunity to buy the shop, which he honestly was selling to me as a hobby and not a viable business.

Now several years later, I still see that brand of frames advertised to consumers who want the rigid steel frame built to their exact specifications. I do not know how the man pays his bills, but the brand lives on, I am certain in large part because building custom steel frames for customers who want that is so much a part of his heart.

This chapter on owning a bike shop or founding a parts company is placed at the point where people have made something of the ultimate commitment for a reason. I have listened to many arguments between spouses as one decides it is time and take the plunge and go into business and the other is wondering where the mortgage payment will come from. Do not fantasize about owning a bike shop. Most fail. If, however, you are ready to take the plunge and make a total dedicated commitment, they can thrive and pay off very well. Do your due diligence and make sound business decisions that are not based solely on your love of cycling.

One possibility would be to work in a shop before buying or starting one. This might seem to be an uneasy fit for people in their thirties or forties, but depending on the market, older people can make more sales. Most bicycles are sold to families and the parents want to know about safety, reliability, service, and value. They do not want to hear stories about weaving through traffic and popping wheelies on a sidewalk. And if you love bicycles, there is nothing like the feeling of selling a new one. You have just given someone the opportunity to live the same happy life you do.

THIRTEEN

Making a Total Commitment to the Bike

There is no time for cut-and-dried monotony. There is time for work.
And there is time for love. That leaves no other time.
—COCO CHANEL

Some people cross the line from recreational use of the bicycle to serious use. After a while they begin to follow racing and cross into the realm of being an avid fan. They have found community, but still need something more. They invest in a shop or a product associated with the bicycle industry, and even take up a bit of racing, yet they are still feeling they need more. These people need to make a total commitment to the bike.

It would be great if so many people fell and stayed in love with another human being and created a marriage as strong as many of these people make with their bikes. I decided to seek these people out and determine why such a total commitment.

I considered first what it means to be totally committed to the bike. I wondered why racers turn pro and ride every day for the cause of the team. For police officers on the bicycle squad, I wanted to know if they rode off-duty and what was it about the bike squad that appealed to them so much. I wondered why a bike messenger would get up every day and subject him or herself to the daily abuse of trucks and cars that would rather run them over than help them complete their jobs. Even worse, why would they subject themselves daily to the extreme weather conditions that can be found in Boston, Minneapolis, or Seattle, or the summer heat of Dallas and Phoenix. I wondered why anyone would dedicate their lives to the elimination of cars with the intent of replacing them with bicycles.

Any one of these people might be considered fanatics, but their experience is what I characterize as total commitment. It is the point at which not only the heart, but the entire physiology cannot live without the bicycle. I am fascinated by this total dedication. This kind of commitment makes for interesting people, people who probably will not die watching television.

I doubt whether any of these people could be considered selfless heroes because they love their bikes, but this total commitment is the beginning of what I believe could be heroism when it is needed. A quick and unscientific survey of people cited for heroism supports my theory.

A young man in Everett, Washington, was cited for heroism by the Everett police for chasing down a purse-snatcher and holding the perpetrator until the police arrived. A young woman witnessed a murder and in spite of several death threats, testified and helped send the murderer to prison for life. Both of these people have chosen to make a total heartfelt commitment to something. I see the same character in the people I interviewed here as I did in the heroes I have known. I believe they would step forward and make a difference when necessary.

I understand why people go to church. There is an inherent need to belong and there is also the inherent need to be part of meaningful practices that cultivate spiritual growth. I have a good voice for singing; I am right on tone and my baritone resonates well in almost any environment. The euphoria I feel after singing easy hymns is not because I like being in church; it's simply because singing makes me feel good.

I also understand why people socialize extensively in bars, parties, and social clubs. They belong to a group, are acknowledged by the group, and participate in the same behavior week after week. Some even feel compelled to participate, just like the most devout adherents to organized religions. The wise may argue the value of either practice, but essentially they are both highly ritualized and achieve the same objective.

In this final chapter I want to profile four people who may seem unconventional to society at large, but fit quite neatly within the cycling community and find their niche among fellow cyclists.

The first, **James MacKay**, is the Bicycle Planner for the City of Denver. The second is **Jesse Card** of Seattle and Everett, Washington, is by his owns words an activist I interviewed via email the night before he set out on the second annual ride4peace from Everett to Washington, D.C. **Michele Swanson** describes her love for bicycles with one simple statement, "I am a bicycle." And the fourth, **Steve Fisher**, is a young cyclo-cross winner.

I chose these four individuals because they represent what most cyclists are, and they live out the true sentiment of this book; they have completely opened their lives and their hearts to the bicycle.

Interview with Michelle Swanson

SR: What was your first bike?

MS: A purple one. It had training wheels that my dad eventually took off.

SR: Did you have tassels on the handlebars?

MS: No. I think as an adult I am going through tassel withdrawal.

MS: My next bike was blue, with a banana seat. When I was ten, my mother found, I don't know where, a mini road bike, which I rode to school.

Michele next acquired a Schwinn Mirada mountain bike. It weighed in at forty pounds and was her bicycle of choice for many years. She related an experience on the Burke Gilman trail where several teenage boys began to chase and harass her. She had ridden some seventy miles on the forty-pound Mirada. Instead of outrunning them, which was near impossible, she jammed on the brakes, knowing they would hit her and the Mirada was heavy and stout enough to survive. Scraped and bruised, Michele did survive along with her bicycle, successfully thwarting the boys.

I asked about her favorite foods. She explained she had spent two years in the Peace Corps in Nicaragua and was happy to eat anything that was not Nicaraguan! She had been a vegetarian for seventeen years before, but while in Nicaragua began to eat meat.

As a starter before a bike ride, she eats oatmeal. After a long ride, she likes "lots of spaghetti with real parmesan cheese; what's up with that fake stuff in the can?"

Michele was reluctant to talk about food. I pressed the issue a bit, and she was forthcoming about having issues with food. These issues were mitigated by cycling, where what she ate was used, and her hunger at the end was not a disorder, but rather a biting reality. She could eat. She could not overeat before riding, as it would ruin the ride, but after and safely. Cycling became crucial to finding a way through these issues.

She added that people with addictive behaviors such as alcoholism can find a way to abstain. They do not need alcohol. But when there is an addiction to food, we cannot abstain; we must eat or we die. Cycling was the tool she used to create a need to eat.

What became apparent during the interview was her familiarity with the bike culture through her mechanics. She noted in particular her trust of the mechanics at The Wheelsmith, formerly in the University district of Seattle. She now rides a customized Rodreguez that was in need of repair at the time of the interview. Her backup was a bike built by friends, starting with a properly sized frame and then built with spare parts from mechanics.

Michele admitted to riding between five and seven thousand miles a year. She claimed that it was necessary to ride at least two hours a day, and if she didn't, she would get an itch inside her bones to ride. Her stint with the Peace Corps in Nicaragua did not offer safe and convenient cycling, so she didn't ride. This lack of cycling caused her to become depressed, and she knew from here on, her life had to be radically thought-through to accommodate cycling, even to the point of making sure any career path she chose would always be in a location where she could safely get on a bike and ride.

I asked her some questions about a bicycling community, and she described her participation in Critical Mass events in Seattle and took great solace in the companionship they offered, but proceeded to describe herself as not social. I explained that many cyclists are either very social and need large groups to ride with, or they are not and predominantly ride alone. Michele finds herself falling into the second category.

I asked Michele is she ever raced, and she found an aversion to the kind of competitiveness found in some people associated with racing. As an undergrad, she had been invited to race for the University of Washington women's racing team, but declined. She explained she does not need to measure herself against other people when cycling. She found the culture of honest competition to be different from the culture of winning at any cost, which includes doping and adopting a hyper-consumerist attitude toward having the absolute latest and lightest equipment. She described it as wanting to be true to cycling.

I finally asked whether cycling was a spiritual, metaphysical, or physiological experience. She settled on calling the experience physiological, describing cycling as being more than from the heart, but as being an intrinsic part of her life. I described for her the various interviews I conducted for this book and the focus again and again on food. She suggested next time I ask cyclists to draw maps, an exercise she used with the people of Nicaragua. The maps would not be of the way home or anything specific, but just maps. We agreed the maps would probably include coffee shops, breakfast joints, steep hills, bike shops, bathrooms, and water supplies.

Interview with Jesse Card

"My name is Jesse Card. I'm twenty-three, am a current resident of Seattle and recent resident of Everett. I wouldn't consider myself an activist. I am, however, politically involved.

"My first involvement in issues was in church-state separation, the environment, civil liberties, and other connected issues.

"I am the plaintiff [in the case] to remove the ten commandments monument from in front of the Police Station and city council chambers of Everett, Washington. The case is currently in appeals. I also ran a farcical campaign for mayor.

"I love the justification you can have for eating delicious and unhealthy food after a long ride. It's hard to be derided for eating a pint of Ben and Jerry's or polish(ing) off a pizza when you're just going to cycle it off the next day.

"I'll be addressing a few of your questions and have sent [them] to others in the group for their responses. I'll be sending along their answers, including [one] from Ron Toppi, the man who thought of and instigated the idea for Bike4Peace.

"Ron's original idea was that using a bicycle shows that you can be independent of the use of an automobile. He definitely believes that the use of oil is a primary reason for our country's current involvement in Iraq. As he's also said in his statement on the website, he is willing to sacrifice certain things in his life to ensure that we won't have to fight (maim, kill) for certain parts of our lives that are unnecessary luxuries. Bikes demonstrate this I think particularly well as they are a device that almost anyone can ride. It needs no license, the chances of you harming anyone else in it are small. It's fairly inexpensive.

"By using a bike, you are throwing off the economic and environmental weights of a car. You're not creating pollution, using non-renewable resources. You're not using a form of transportation that makes people move farther from each other, more isolated, less inclined to growing community.

"Most people, with only a little education, can learn to maintain and repair most aspects of their bike. This is also less expensive than in an auto.

"Ron Toppi, before doing Bike4Peace, first started and managed Sharing Wheels, a community bike shop in Everett, Washington (sharingwheels.org). The purpose of doing so was to make bikes available and affordable for anyone. You can come into his shop and pay just a few dollars for parts or a repair. Ideally, you'll stop and learn how to do it yourself. He also takes donated bikes, refurbishes and repairs them, and sells them at much more affordable prices. There's also the option to work for your bike.

"Through the work for bike programs, you learn how to build, repair, and maintain your bicycle. Making you more independent as you now not only own a bicycle, but know how to maintain and repair it, avoiding excessive labor fees in a conventional bike shop.

"Many of our group take time away from work and family not because of conditions enabling them to, but in spite of. Jeff, who joined us on our first trip last year, had been recently homeless for three years and in transitional housing. Ron works at lower-wage jobs that he finds more personally rewarding, and generally spends his days 'off' volunteering at Sharing Wheels.

"As for myself, I've been working toward a lower-maintenance and less consumerist lifestyle. I'm trying to live a fulfilling life, have time for myself, and have a low impact on the environment. I have gone through training and have the knowledge to be installing solar hot water and electric systems, but have not yet begun to do so, in some part due to the need for a vehicle in that field. I live in group houses where we often share food. I dumpster a fair portion of my food and many belongings and reuse or repair as much as possible. I'm just trying to get out of the 'consume, consume!' lifestyle.

"So, my point was, we're not upper-middle-income people who can actually afford to take this time off. I spent the rest of the year saving and am currently concerned about the cost of filling cavities that I was told I have last time I was in the dentist. We're not rich, just dedicated. One of us is an anarchist, and most of us left-leaning on all issues, if not economic. I think, compared to the current thinking on how you should live, bikes are far more affordable and we take actions towards getting them even more available to people of lower incomes, including Everett's homeless population. If you need something faster than walking, biking is your best option. We'd like communities to be built less towards the car, but more towards walking, thus eliminating the need for any form of transportation to further ensure the quality of life for those in poverty and lower incomes.

"I'm not sure we would identify as cyclists. I wouldn't. For most of the group this will be the first long ride of their lives.

"My own story on that: Last year, I wasn't sure about the ride. About a month and a half before, the meetings for this action were in the basement of my work. A friend (and current rider) Vernon would give me updates. One day he wasn't there and so one of our supporters, Lorna, filled me in. Afterward she asked 'Why? Are you one of the riders?' I expressed scoffing amazement at the idea, but it's when my wheels first started to turn.

Could I do that? Maybe. Yeah, I could do that. Well, if I can, I will.

"And so I expressed my interest to Ron, but my dismay at not having an adequate bike. He set me up with a bike and I started training.

"I hadn't ridden my bike in six months, and when I had it was 11 blocks every two weeks for laundry. I'd never ridden more than five miles before this. So I started training, and worked up to a longest day distance of forty-two miles. Still far short of our average of eighty-two miles a day. However, I think this was great proof that anyone could ride their bike if they had the will, even across the country.

"I told almost all of our hosts this story along the way. Many had expressed, 'I couldn't ride my bike five miles, let alone across the country!' Give'm food for thought.

"So I don't consider myself a cyclist, just someone who will for a variety of social, environmental, and financial reasons, use a bike for most of my transportation needs. Cyclist has too many recreational connotations. I frown on the marketing of bikes for recreation only. I've often expressed frustration with our local Cascade Bicycle Club for riding their SUVs to a trail to ride their three-thousand-dollar bikes, so long as it isn't raining. I'd rather they were used for getting around town. As a main form of transportation.

Another member of the ride4peace group responded with this:

"War is not the result of a single person or even a small cabal's actions. Most of us are complicit in various ways. Besides electing the leaders and paying our taxes, we may work for the military industrial complex or buy products that require the resources (like oil) over which wars are fought.

"The bicycle is the most efficient way to transport a human being, in terms of total energy spent. Bicycles are an elegantly appropriate technology.

"Do you really know somebody who cannot afford a bicycle? Community bike shops recycle used cycles and often trade for volunteer labor from people who have no cash. Because of their efficiency, bicycles quickly pay for themselves in transportation savings.

"We're just ordinary people, not extraordinary athletes. But we'd rather get around without cars than kill for oil. We're hoping others will realize that, if we can ride across country, they can ride across town.

"Raised a pacifist, I've been politically active all my fifty years.

"I lean toward a raw vegan diet, when it's available, but don't like to define myself by limitations. Cantaloupe, avocado, spinach, broccoli, yams, turnips, sprouts, wheatgrass, walnuts, spirolina, kombucha and soy yogurt are among my favorites. Ginger, ginseng, garlic, lemongrass and a good curry keep food interesting. In a pinch, I'll eat bugs."

Interview with James Mackay, Bicycle Planner, City of Denver

James Mackay, P.E., is the Bicycle Planner for the City of Denver. Our interview was on the day before Denver was planning to reinforce the speed limit on the bicycle path in Washington Park. One of his main concerns was the value of cyclists also observing the law as a means of reducing antagonism between themselves and motorists.

James's first bike was a Triumph Rodeo, a single-speed with coaster brakes. It was originally painted red, but after many years of use had dulled and scratched. It was his main ride to school in the third grade and beyond in 1964.

He rides in excess of five thousand miles a year, to and from the office and then as the bicycle planner out to various parts of the city as the paths and streets are built, upgraded and maintained. On the weekends, he rides his mountain bike for a change from the street potholes and the maniac drivers.

I asked about his experiences of road rage and how one might mitigate that experience and reduce the risk of harm. He first clarified he is an engineer and not a psychologist. He can post pleasant and informative signage asking motorists to share the road, but once they get behind the wheel it is a law enforcement and a social psychological issue: how to convince people to get along. The police can punish violators of the law, but it might take more than that in the long term.

For the number of years he has been commuting in Denver, he has learned a few tricks that reduce the rage. First, he observes the law. When the lights indicate slowing to a stoplight, he slows and stops right next to the vehicles. He has often witnessed cyclists speeding up and blowing through stop lights, and he can clearly see the anger in the faces of motorists who are legally stopped and waiting, or who are cut off by this flagrant violation of the law.

When riding among pedestrians, he is careful to observe those laws as well, especially as they pertain to riding a bike on the sidewalk. When riding on a trail, a polite ring of a bell and a thank you as he passes wide around the pedestrian usually gets a thank you in return, rather than the cursing he witnesses when aggressive cyclists pass to closely, yell at pedestrians or, even worse, run them off the path. No wonder some people hate cyclists.

In Denver, these types of cyclists have been known as Scorchers since the 1890s. He acknowledged that the 2003 revised plan does try to separate the various kinds of cyclists and noted he was pleased the law enforcement would begin in Washington Park. He was also concerned about speeding cyclists in the city where there is limited or obstructed sight. In several areas of the trail, there is limited sight because of cresting hills, ninety degree turns under bridges and natural obstacles that a cyclist should slow down for. He noted there are a number of accidents on the city paths and streets directly associated with speeding into sight-obstructed areas.

The bicycle is more than his job, even though his job demonstrates a total commitment to making cycling available and safer for the citizens of Denver. His recollection of riding to school past the orange groves as they blossomed is something he could never replicate in a car. Driving the car through the orchards he likened to watching a nature show on a big-screen television. We talked a bit about what he referred to the "milk-carton children," those who suffer at the hands of predators. There is not a lot that even a well-planned bicycle path can do to prevent abductions, except put the child in a safe and visible area of the street. Using well-marked and well-traveled paths might mitigate this problem and allow children to get on their bikes and ride to school. I suggested a patrol of retired persons who need their daily bike rides and can serve in the same capacity as crosswalk guards; they can be the watchful eyes along the bicycle paths leading to local grade and middle schools. He liked the idea.

James described himself as a fan of the "crank and plank," something that happens frequently in Denver. He is both a cyclist and a skier. He admitted this in the context of our discussion about his favorite foods. His most favorite food is Aimée's organic spinach pizza, which he supplements with green peppers, olives, garlic, and two inches of cheddar cheese. In addition to bicycling, he belongs to a ski club, where he raised a lot of eyebrows among the women when they discovered he could cook.

After long rides, his second-most favorite food is nachos, made with organic blue corn chips, black beans, olives, and cheddar cheese that he piles usually about six to seven inches high. He has decided to go back to cooking lasagna because now with the organic no-bake noodle, he can cook lasagna in an easy twenty minutes and satisfy a post-ride hunger quickly. The easiest post-ride food he can fix is whole wheat bread, organic butter, organic almond butter, strawberry jelly, and some red wine.

What does he carry in his pack? Optimum bars and Larabars. He prefers the Cherry Pie Larabar, a concoction made locally in Denver.

Interview with Steve Fisher, Cyclo-Cross Winner

Steve is a sixteen-year-old high school student living in Lynn-wood, Washington. At first sight, this quiet, unassuming young man just blends in. But once you consider the fact he placed second in the Junior Nationals in Cyclo-cross, you notice something different.

I asked Steve when he first competed in a bicycle race. He took his mountain bike to a junior cyclo-cross race when he was thirteen. Did he win? Steve smiled and said he finished. He wasn't sure if he finished dead last, but it was something like that.

He said his first bike was some kind of bike with solid tires, he didn't remember the brand. His first serious ride was with his parents when they took him, at age thirteen, on the RSVP ride from Seattle to Vancouver, B.C. His mother indicated that between the complaints she fed him candy, and he finished the ride. He subsequently rode the Seattle to Portland ride in two days, again with his parents. By then, he agreed he was hooked on cycling.

I have followed Steve's racing through the newspapers and websites detailing local race results. I have long wondered how people become so positively focused on success at such a young age. I asked Steve if he had always been a competitive person and he quickly said no, but he got a taste of it when he began to compete seriously in swimming. Once he knew he could compete and win, that became the focus of his competition.

The Seattle area is known for its glorious summers and wretched winters. If you train for any outdoor competition in Seattle, you train in miserable conditions. I asked Steve why he gets on his bike in the middle February when it's thirty-six degrees and raining. His answer was quick: so he could focus on winning at Nationals, and not just come in second. I dug a little deeper. Training every day, and especially training in the cold on steep hills, begins to hurt. Why endure the pain, and the answer was the same—so he could win at Nationals and not come in second.

We all have people around us who are convinced we won't succeed and make it a point to tell us so every time we try something new. Some people are affected by this negativity that gets into their heads and they fail. Steve assured me there are people like that near him, and he simply blows them off. I asked if he has something to prove to them, and he said he's in this for himself. He has nothing to prove to them.

I asked Steve if, other than his parents, coaches and teachers, there was a larger-than-life person whose actions or accomplishments motivate him to succeed, and he said no. He repeated that he's in it for himself. He motivates himself.

Steve indicated he is open to a professional career in racing. His former cycling coach just signed a professional contract in Europe, and he agreed that is a worthy goal to shoot for. His options are open, though, and he plans on attending college— albeit a college with a serious cycling program.

I asked Steve about his favorite all-time food (lasagna) and favorite school cafeteria food (vanilla pudding). What does he eat before a race? Strawberry oatmeal.

I finally asked Steve what advice he would give to younger aspiring cyclists just entering the junior circuit. He said they should just get out and ride a lot, enter races, and not care if they win: Just get out there and ride.

FOURTEEN

Today a Bike Path, Tomorrow the World

Imagine an international spy given the task of infiltrating an organization dedicated to turning this country into a "velonation," a world where only bicycles are used for transportation.. I am not sure the book would sell, nor would Sean Connery be much interested in the starring role when the movie came out. The plot would inevitably include some heart racing chase scenes through, say, San Francisco, on bicycle. Cut away to a scene in a dinghy warehouse in downtown Seattle as various subversive organizations plot together to promote cycling. Imagine all of this amidst the smell of rubber tires, chain oil, and sweat.

The scenario is humorous at best with little substance. The so-called subversive organizations at their worst use one or two cyclists to "cork" traffic as hundreds of cyclists go through intersections against the red lights.

What is gaining momentum, though, is studying the growth of cycling and the effects it has on local, national, and international economies. Capturing dollars for facilities that promote cycling in a world with fewer dollars to commit contributes considerably to the curiosity, as well as a genuine interest in raising awareness of cycling and demonstrating the economic clout of the sport.

The Earth Policy Institute in 2005 posted information on their web site www.earth-policy.org regarding the production of bicycles world wide. In 1950, there were about ten million bicycles produced world wide. In 2003, that number rose to over 105 million. The most number of cars produced in a single year was 42 million.

China continues to produce the largest number, producing almost 73 million bicycles in 2003. They exported 51 million of these, mostly to the United States. China is responsible for seventy percent of world bicycle production.

These figures are interesting when one considers that Europe remains the leader in world bicycle use. In Amsterdam alone, the Earth Policy Institute claims thirty percent of all trips are completed on a bicycle and in Copenhagen, more than thirty percent of workers commute by bicycle. Amsterdam has designed traffic laws that require cars to travel at the same speed as cyclists in what are known as *woonerf* zones. London introduced a congestion tax that ultimately caused automobile traffic to decrease and bicycle traffic to increase.

The United States imports the lion share of bicycles, yet the Europeans and Chinese ride them. This is perhaps a reflection on our affluence and not necessarily on our lack of interest in cycling. I own four bicycles that are designed for specific uses: road training, cyclocross, mountain biking and track racing. I may not need four bicycles, but I use each different bike enough for my own justification.

The growing demand for bicycles is good news for bicycle shops, whether the buyers ever use them or not. Earlier in this book I noted that large corporations were required to reduce the number of automobile commute trips, and one of the tactics used is to encourage bicycle commuting. The health and economic benefits are easy to comprehend. This activity, however, also encourages cyclists to participate in cleaning the air, reducing noise, and improving road congestion. It does little for the large corporations.

Recent studies have shown that approaching the issue of cycling from a different perspective will result in positive economic impacts. The Institute for Transportation Research and Education at North Carolina State University studied the positive economic impact of bicycle facilities in the outer Banks region. The results of this study can be found on the www.americantrails.org web site.

Over the past ten years, almost seven million dollars of public funds were spent on building and improving bicycle facilities in the Outer Banks region. The result, according to the study, is an influx of over sixty million dollars into the region as a direct result of public use of the facilities. Tourists have cited the existence of these extensive facilities as the reason they chose to visit the Outer Banks. More than seventeen percent of all tourist visitors to the Outer Banks were cyclists. The study also indicates 1,400 full-time and seasonal jobs depend on tourists using the bicycle facilities.

A study completed by George Street research of London concluded that in 2003 almost 300,000 trips were made to the Highlands region of England specifically for cycling. When counting in all other niche tourists activities such as hiking, mountaineering, snow sports, and fishing, there were almost 500,000 trips to the Highlands region, accounting for 613 full-time employees dedicated to niche tourism in the region. This study can be found at www.hie.co.uk by searching under "niche-tourism."

The web site www.vistituscon.org, offers some interesting statistics on the economic impact of local bicycle racing events. The El Tour de Tucson is an event open to professional and amateur cyclists alike, and it is estimated the event will bring 13 to 18 million dollars on one weekend alone and will generate over 40 million dollars year round. The USTA Winter Championships in January of 2007 are anticipated to bring in over two million dollars for that single event.

Clearly cycling is having a very positive economic impact as people choose what the British call niche tourism, specifically cycling. It is noted in all of these studies tourists are looking for fun and healthy activities, and specifically target regions that have made an investment in facilities such as trails, safety programs, shower and change facilities, and designated roadways. Following this investment comes the benefit to local hotels, restaurants, bicycle shops, and other tourist activities.

I was invited to share the air waves with an engineer from a Seattle suburb during a local radio talk show. He was adamant bicycles were for children and should be relegated to minimal pathways used exclusive for family recreation. The economic impact of cycling, however, as a chosen pursuit for tourism and serious recreation by adults clearly demonstrates the opposite is true. I suggest local communities with an abundance of natural beauty but little economic opportunity look at the minimal investment required to build up bicycle facilities, advertise these improvements, and let the tourist dollars roll in.

In keeping with the focus and intent of this book and the family of books in this series, I want to explore also what this might bring to the individual. I have covered a lot of ground in this book, from buying a first bike, through conditioning, diet, commuting and racing. Beyond racing and owning a bicycle shop, the ultimate commitment to cycling is serving as a larger-than-life community advocate that recognizes the power of the cycling dollar and the benefit to the local community of encouraging quiet, healthy recreational activities. Now that is a total commitment to cycling.

An Interview
With Steve Fisher

I was able to catch up again with Steve Fisher well into the new school year as well the Fall 2006 cyclocross season. Before we went to press, I was able to ask Steve a few more questions, mostly focused on the progress he is making toward repeating or improving his number two finish in Junior Nationals.

Shawn Rohrbach (SR): You have been racing with the A men locally in this 2006 cross season. Why were you placed in this category? Was there a lack of competition within your age category? Did they think you were sandbagging? What does it feel like competing against that age group? Are you intimidated by it?

Steve Fisher (SF): I have chosen to race that category for the challenge of it and there simply is no competition for me within the junior categories. There are a few of us that are simply much faster. Racing with the men also helps to better prepare us for the bigger races. We could race juniors if we wanted to, but we choose not to. Sometimes it can be intimidating. Sometimes the older riders have a lack of respect for us, but when we race well and produce results respect is earned. I know how to bump and use my elbows when I need to. It is cool racing with the fastest group of men because it shows me how far I am from the very top.

SR: The elite juniors you are racing with now nationally, will these be the competitors you race against in nationals? Are you considered an elite junior now?

SF: Yes, they are the same as those that will be at nationals. The USGP series is a six-race nationals cross series. There is one weekend in Mass, one in CO, and one here in the NW. All of the races are UCI sanctioned. The series is used for selection to the World Championship team. I am considered an elite junior now. An "elite junior" is just a rider with a racing age of 17 or 18.

SR: The last time we talked, you noted your training schedule was fairly consistent through the summer. Were you able to keep up the same intensity when your school year started? Are you doing anything differently this fall than you did last year?

SF: I am able to keep the intensity up when school starts, but sometimes I have to scale back the volume. It takes some adjusting once school starts, but after a few weeks I settle into a routine. Once daylight savings time starts I have to make sure and get on the bike right after school to finish before dark. Training is fairly similar to last year, but maybe with more rest because all of the big weekends and traveling take their toll.

SR: Last summer when we talked, you indicated that obviously you would pursue college and hopefully race during that time. I noticed the scholarship program at Colorado State for cyclists. Have you looked into that?

SF: I haven't looked into that specifically. I do plan on going to college in either Washington or Colorado. If I go to CO it would be for some sort of cycling program. A scholarship would just make it even better.

SR: The Olympics are coming in 2008, two racing seasons away. Are you aware of how you might be able to join the US team and are you even interested this time around? Six years from now, the 2012 Olympics will be in London. Is that a goal? As a sports reporter in high school, I asked this question of a classmate who was competitively skiing, and he had not seriously thought about it, but after I asked him the question he ended up at the Olympic training center in Colorado and went to the 1976 games as a member of the US team.

SF: I can't say that the Olympics are a goal of mine. Sure it would be really cool and all. Cyclocross is not yet an Olympic sport, but of course road, track and mountain bike racing are. The OTC has a focus on track racing. Probably because there are numerous events which equal more medal opportunities. A better option would be the U23 national road team that races in Europe.

SR: Are you sticking to cyclocross or do you have the ambition to race road and track as well, and will you be pursuing that this next spring and summer?

SF: Cyclocross is definitely my favorite, but I have been racing full seasons of road as well. My plans for this spring/summer begin with a late start after a rest from the cross season. Then I plan on racing mostly crits, but also some track racing, and maybe some mountain bike racing as well.

SR: Finally, have you been approached by other teams or are you happy to be with Oberto?

SF: I'm actually racing for Rad Racing NW. I was on Oberto last year. The local Jr teams try not to recruit riders from other teams, so it is really up to the rider about which team they ride for. Of course the team has to want to have the rider. Some adult road teams have shown interest in me, but even then they sort of wait until a rider is eighteen before seriously recruiting them.

Conclusion

It is perhaps difficult to understand why people use the bicycle to achieve a mastery of life, or if that it is even possible: Until you ride like it is your love for life at stake. People find that cycling is the very thing that opens all the doors and allows them to feel truly alive, or it is part of a larger effort that includes many pursuits and practices. Some will give up on it altogether and pursue something else, and the valuable lesson there is to pursue something.

What is clear after considering this from several angles and speaking with many people about cycling is that cycling works. It opens up passions, awakens the mind and heart, energizes the soul, and renews physical wellness.

Any activity that not only burns excess calories but demands an intake of more is worthy of consideration. This is not because we are in an image conscious culture where thin is in, but because cycling actually utilizes the body the way it was meant to be.

Muscles were given to us to exercise. We do not live in an agrarian society where we need to push plows and till the soil, and we are beyond the mechanical and industrial ages where our muscles were used to shaped steel and wood. We still have muscles, however, and once we utilize them properly in a healthy fashion, they grow and we feel the benefits of strength.

We also make society stronger by cycling. We all have a desire to be recognized for our charitable or socially conscious works, and there is something deeply satisfying about contributing less to air pollution and road rage and more to a quieter, gentler manner of getting to work. We contribute to a process that passes a cleaner environment and a more peaceful existence on to our children.

If this is as far as most people get with cycling, they have accomplished a more holistic use of their bodies and have given something back to society. Many choose to go beyond and more deeply embrace the bicycle as part of their mastery.

The commitment to live a life devoted to making cycling more available and safer for everyone from children to the most elite racers takes on many faces. People design bicycles and parts, and wholesalers sell them to shop owners who connect people to the bike. Urban planners take over from there and design safer pathways for recreation, training, and commuting. The social advocates enter the picture and raise awareness about the presence of bicycles and their benefit to society. In turn, most cyclists give back to this process by honoring the intent and letter of the law. Examining the total number of people positively affected, as well as the number and complexity of these relationships, is fascinating.

I have avoided the topic of performance-enhancing drugs and professional athletes in this book for good purpose. The people I have met in my research have no desire to take them. They ride because it is a pure practice, whether the end result is just a little exercise, a slower more peaceful commute, or a total life long commitment. They all accomplish a similar goal: they open their hearts to something like cycling and sit back and count the benefits. The topic of these drugs, though, is worth a serious look. I always wonder why people sell out the pure form of something for short-term gain. Another book, perhaps.

The four interviews I conducted while writing this book were the most rewarding part. After putting out mild feelers for information from people who loved cycling, I received many very passionate responses and selected the members of bike4peace, Michele Swanson, John MacKay, and Steve Fisher to interview. Each interview offered a unique perspective on cycling, none more devoted than another. The people I interviewed offered exactly what I was looking for: infectious enthusiasm about a terrific sport.

Steve Fisher might have summed it up best: get on your bike and ride.

APPENDIX ONE

Favorite Recipes

Here are a few of the foods my family enjoys, some of which have sustained me now for over fifty years. Some of these recipes were developed to feed our guests at the Haus Rohrbach Pensione in Leavenworth, Washington, specifically the breakfast items. I make no apologies for the level of carbohydrates in these recipes and actually embrace them. Before recreating these recipes, please consider your own capacity for cholesterol, sugar, and fats.

BREAKFAST

RÖSTI

Serves 8–10 as a side or complementary dish.

2¼ lbs. waxy potatoes
Salt and pepper
4 T. butter
2 t. oil

Boil the potatoes until just tender. Drain and leave overnight. Next day peel and grate them coarsely and season with salt and pepper. Heat half the butter and oil in a heavy frying pan and press the potatoes into a small cake. Cook over moderate heat for about twenty minutes, or until the bottom is golden brown and crusty. Invert the rösti onto a plate. Heat the rest of the butter and oil in the pan, slide the rösti back into the pan and cook the other side, about ten minutes more. No catsup, please!

OVEN OMELET

Serves 4–8 adults

8 eggs
1 cup milk
$\frac{1}{2}$ t. seasoned salt
1 cup chopped zucchini
$\frac{1}{2}$ cup crisp bacon pieces or cubed ham
1 cup sautéed mushrooms
Grated Parmesan cheese

Preheat over to 325 degrees. Beat together eggs, milk, and seasoned salt. Add zucchini, meat, and mushrooms. Pour into greased 8 x 8 x 2 pan. Spread generously with parmesan cheese (substitute other cheeses to taste). Bake uncovered 40–45 minutes or until the omelet is set and top is golden brown. This dish allows several people to enjoy the omelet at the same time rather than cooking individual omelets.

CRANBERRY-ORANGE SCONES

Makes 12 scones
(cyclists are known, however, to eat several at a sitting)

1 cup flour
1 cup cake flour
$\frac{2}{3}$ cup sugar
2 t. baking powder
$\frac{1}{2}$ t. salt
3 T. chilled stick margarine or butter, cut up
$\frac{3}{4}$ cup dried cranberries
2 t. grated orange rind
$\frac{3}{4}$ cup plain yogurt
2 t. sugar

Combine first six ingredients in a bowl. Cut in margarine with pastry blender or two knives until the mixture resembles coarse meal. Add cranberries and orange rind, toss well. Add yogurt, stirring until dry ingredients are moistened. Dough will be very sticky. Turn dough out on a floured surface, and with floured hands, knead four or five times. Pat dough into a large circle on a baking sheet coated with cooking spray. Cut dough into twelve wedges, but do not separate the wedges yet. Sprinkle the 2 teaspoons of sugar over dough. Bake at 350 degrees for 20 minutes or until golden. Get some coffee ready!

BLUEBERRY COFFEE CAKE

Serves 6–10
(unless I find it freshly baked just after cycling)

CAKE
$^3\!/_4$ cup sugar
$^1\!/_4$ cup soft shortening
1 egg
$^1\!/_2$ cup milk
2 cups flour
2 t. baking powder
$^1\!/_2$ t. salt
2 cups well-drained blueberries
(Go pick wild blueberries for the best-tasting cake!)

Heat over to 375 degrees. Grease and flour a 9 x 9 x 1$^3\!/_4$ flat pan. Mix sugar, shortening, and egg thoroughly. Stir in milk. Blend dry ingredients, stir in. Blend the blueberries in last. Spread batter in pan. Sprinkle with topping (see below). Bake 45–50 minutes.

TOPPING
$^1\!/_2$ cup sugar
$^1\!/_3$ cup flour
1 t. cinnamon
$^1\!/_4$ cup soft butter

Blend with pastry blender. This should yield nine 3-inch squares, but I have been known to polish off an entire pan by myself after a long ride. Get more coffee.

FRIED APPLES

Serves 2–10
My personal favorite for holiday breakfasts.

*2–10 large apples, depending on the number of people;
about 1 apple per person*

*4–12 slices of bacon, cooked, dried and crumbled.
1–2 slices per person, or as your diet permits.*

1 t. oil

Cut apples into thin slices. Keep the skin on if you desire. Place apple slices and oil in heavy frying pan. Sprinkle generously with cinnamon and sugar to taste. Stir a few times as the apples cook down and release moisture. You might be tempted to add water, but there is enough moisture in the apples. Cooking time can be as short as five minutes or as long as fifteen minutes, depending on the size of the recipe. During the last two turns, fold in the bacon bits.

NANA'S CINNAMON BREAD

2–4 loaves, depending on the size of the pans

4 cups milk

2 pkgs. yeast, dissolved

1½ T. salt

¾ cup sugar

½ cup butter

3 eggs, beaten

Flour*

* If you have made bread before, you know how much. If not, maybe make
some basic bread first to learn, or just wing it and see what happens.
Or try www.breadinfo.com for additional information.

Create a "mixture" of butter, sugar, and cinnamon. (This will go inside the loaf, so make it as sweet and thick as you like, just don't tell your doctor about it.)

Heat the milk, salt, sugar and butter in a medium saucepan. Let it cool and then add the flour, eggs, and yeast mixture, alternating, but start and end with the flour. Bread-makers, you already know how to do this. After the dough rises once, punch it down and place on a floured board and knead the dough, adding more flour as needed until it is not sticky. Divide it into the desire loaf size (4 regular or 8 mini). Roll each loaf out into a rectangular shape and brush with the "mixture." Roll up and set loaf in greased pan to rise again. Bake at 350 degrees for 20–25 minutes. Brush each loaf lightly with butter and sprinkle with sugar after removing loaf from oven. (Serve toasted and buttered with coffee or fresh milk.)

CINNAMON ROLLS

Makes 10–12 large rolls

Start with the basic dough from Nana's Cinnamon Bread. Once the dough has risen twice, roll all of the dough into an elongated rectangle. Using the "mixture" and raisins, generously cover the dough. Roll the dough into one long roll and cut the roll into 2–3-inch rolls, placing them face up in a greased pan. Bake at 350 degrees for 20–25 minutes. Create or buy a powdered sugar frosting and after the rolls have cooled, cover generously with frosting. (You will have to regulate the number your fellow cyclists can each eat)

LUNCH

You're on your own.

DINNER

PUMPKIN-APPLE SOUP

Makes 4 generous servings

1 T. butter or margarine
1 T. finely chopped onion, more if you like onions as much as I do
1 large Granny Smith apple; coarse-grated or fine-chopped
1 cup cooked pumpkin, substitute with canned if necessary
3 cups chicken broth
1 t. curry powder
Salt to taste
white pepper to taste
4 T. shelled roasted pumpkin seeds
chives for flavor

In a medium saucepan, melt butter over medium heat. Add onion. Sauté until softened; do not brown. Add apple, pumpkin, broth, and curry. Season with salt and white pepper. Bring to a boil. Reduce heat. Cover and simmer; stir occasionally for 25 minutes or until apple and onion are tender. Reheat if necessary. Sprinkle each serving with a few pumpkin seeds and garnish with chives. (This is a fast and easy way to take the edge off of a long, cold autumn ride!)

COUNTRY CASSEROLE

Serves 10–12 people
*This recipe was developed for feeding a cycling team,
an army platoon, or my family on Sunday.*

3 lbs lean hamburger

1/2 cup onions

3 cloves of garlic

1/2 cup Karo corn syrup or 1/4 cup molasses

8 oz.-can tomato sauce

1/4 cup vinegar

1 T. Worcester sauce

1 T. mustard

2 t. salt

1/4 t. pepper

1/4 t. oregano (or to taste for flavor)

*1 large can whole tomatoes
(fresh tomatoes can be used, of course,
but the whole canned tomatoes are peeled)*

*2 cups shredded or cut-up cheese
(experiment with the kinds you like)*

egg noodles (usually one whole bag).

Boil noodles until tender, mix and sauté other ingredients together until hamburger is brown. Hold back the cheese until you mix together with noodles and sautéed meat in large casserole and bake for 1 hour at 350.

APPENDIX TWO

Off-Season Training

Once winter begins to get serious, bicycles are usually stored and promises are made to get an early start in the spring. The more dedicated continue to ride through inclement weather and the creative stay in condition by choosing other sports or taking vacation time to sunnier, warmer climes. Whatever the path, developing an off-season training plan will help prevent the need for long term conditioning when the next season begins to open up.

Lifelong athletes already have their off-season plans in place. I am anxious for the first flakes of snow to appear and add to my training a program more suited for winter sports. I recommend other books in this series for an in-depth look at training, skiing, basketball, and other activities that can be done during the winter, either indoors or out.

The focus of this chapter will be a consideration of how to continue a cycling program through the winter months even if you are not a highly paid professional cyclist who can afford to live in Spain, Australia, or South Africa.

If you live north of the Mason-Dixon in the US, you know about wind, rain, snow, ice storms, lake-effect snow from Illinois to New Hampshire, the Pineapple Express in the Northwest, and our little friend, black ice, on bridges and overpasses. Riding a bicycle in this is usually not recommended.

A member of an amateur cycling team in Seattle was enjoying a late fall ride recently and slipped on a pile of wet leaves that had not been removed from the trail. He suffered multiple fractures.

The bicycle trails in Boulder, Colorado, are scraped clean usually after every snow, but that did not prevent my own mishap on a patch of black ice. I suffered a small fracture in my hip and spent New Year's 2000 in bed.

During a recent snow storm in Seattle, a man in his thirties was picking his way around piles of snow and patches of ice and through clogged traffic. I waved him over to my car as I waited for the traffic to move another inch and asked him if he was comfortable riding in the snow. He responded with a laugh. First, he had fallen several times, but was not hurt. Second, he had been able to get to work and run errands in about the same time most of his colleagues had spent getting from their homes down to the freeway and back home. He pedaled off slowly around stalled cars and off to a dinner date he intended to make.

Cycling in the extremes of either hemisphere during the winter months can prove problematic. Of all these cities, Seattle and Vancouver offer the most mild winters and most dedicated cyclists can easily ride twelve months a year. I wonder how many cyclists in Rochester, New York, or Portland, Maine, can boast the same.

Fortunately, there are alternatives for those who choose not to take up skiing, basketball or other sports more acclimated for winter months.

In-door Trainers

Some people cringe at the thought of pedaling a bike and going no where. Others swear by it. The idea is simple; clamp the bike into a device that allows the cyclist to pedal and causes various levels of resistance. Those who are dedicated to this type of winter training plan out material to read and movies and sporting events they can watch on a television while they train. Some simply plug their MP3 device into their ears and catch up on the latest music. Competitive cyclists use in-door trainers not only off-season, but during the season as well to warm up for a race.

There are several different types of in-door trainers that offer different types of resistance at different price levels.

The most common are the wind trainers. The resistance comes from a fan that is turned by the bicycle wheel. There is an adjustment knob that allows the cyclist to increase the pressure of the roller on the wheel and therefore the resistance. While these are affordable, they can be noisy. There is little that can be done to quiet the noise. I use a wind trainer outside under my patio awning and the noise does not bother any one. I would advise testing this type of trainer if you must train inside an apartment or condominium with neighbors just one wall away.

Mag trainers use magnetic fields for generating resistance. These are quiet and can offer a wider range of resistance options. While these are priced higher, they offer the cyclist the option of training close to other people. Several friends of mine train while they watch television with the family. Some models offer automatic tension adjustments based on the amount of effort exerted.

The quietest and smoothest of the portable trainers is a fluid trainer that generates hydraulic resistance using internal fluids.

There are several videos offering anything from scenery to simulate a bicycle ride to professional level fitness training for racing. This helps the cyclist focus on the training and not the latest DVD rental.

Finally, for many years competitive cyclists have used rollers that are the closest simulation of actually riding on a smooth surface. This model lays flat on the floor and the cyclist simply mounts and starts riding, the rear wheel set between two rollers and the front wheel set flat on one roller. The cyclist can simulate mild spinning up to extreme sprinting.

When asked what kind of trainer someone should buy, I respond by asking what they are willing to pay. If they have a small budget, I tell them to get a wind trainer, and if they can afford more, then the mag or fluid trainers offer more options and do not create a racket. The bottom line, however, is if someone has a lot of reading material or needs to catch up on the movies they didn't see all summer, a trainer is a great in-door option for the winter.

Spinning Classes

Most higher-end health clubs offer classes in spinning. They use positive motion trainers that operate much like a track bike; there is only forward motion and no back pedaling. The trainers usually have some adjustment knob that increases tension and therefore resistance on the flywheel.

Spinning classes last anywhere from thirty to ninety minutes, depending on the level of fitness of the participants. There are strong opinions of the usefulness of these classes and the root of this debate is in the style of the trainer. Some trainers develop routines for the classes that focus on overall fitness, where others emphasize bicycle racing and yet others focus on glamour muscles. Trainers with a large following have tapped into the needs and wants of the club clientele and offer the type of training these paying customers want. Some trainers don't last long because they have developed the wrong program or they do not have the kind of personality paying customers want to listen to.

When looking for a spinning class in a club, ask if you can join the class for a free session. Of course the sales people want you to sign up today, but using a spinning class for off-season training is a big and often expensive commitment. Choose wisely.

The Risks of Cold Weather Training

Early last spring, I had to drop off a vehicle and I thought this would be a great opportunity to get an easy twenty-five mile ride for an early start on my out door training. I had been riding all winter when it wasn't raining and had been able to train on my bike outdoors all twelve months of the year. For Seattle, this is not such a great achievement, but still I am always happy when I can accomplish this. Typically I tend to over-dress for the winter and shed the layers as I warm up. On this Saturday, I believed the weather forecast and headed out wearing enough protection for the predicted forty-eight degrees with no precipitation.

Beyond the point of no return on my ride, a small, freak cold front moved across a narrow band of Washington State. In minutes I was soaking wet and was then treated to a high wind and hail. One might think the smart thing to do would be to camp out in a coffee shop for a few hours or call home. The website sports medicine.about. com lists the symptoms of hypothermia, and the most dangerous among them is confusion. A person suffering from severe hypothermia sometimes even thinks they are over heating. I almost reached that point, and I was definitely not making sound judgments. Instead of pulling off and drying out in a restaurant or even a laundromat, both of which were accessible, I pressed on for the last ten miles to my other vehicle. Looking back on the incident, I do not recall, even after formal training in methods of survival and having spent fifty years in many severely cold regions, even thinking of these techniques. I just kept riding.

Fifty percent of your body heat can escape through head protection that is inadequate for the weather. My scalp cover under my helmet was wet and was sucking the heat out of my body. When I finally got my car to my gym, my feet were numb, and I am told I did not stop at the front desk to show my membership card. I got into the sauna and after a few minutes awakened to what I had just put myself through.

Every source of medical advice I was able to find lists some common essentials for cold weather training that will help avoid hypothermia and frostbite.

- Dress in layers

- Cover the head and if this covering becomes wet, change it.

- Wear clothing that wicks the water away. Almost every major sport shop will carry such garments.

- Eat enough food and drink a lot of water even if it appears you are not thirsty in the wet, cold weather.

- Do not drink alcohol. As much as we think a few shots of brandy will warm us up, it actually cools the body and increases the risk of hypothermia.

- Cover hands, legs, and even the face if the temperature drops precipitously.

- Carry a change of clothing, especially of garments closest to the body.

Visit your local bike shop and talk about the clothing they have for winter training. Don't cheap out. Buy the proper scalp covering, shoe and ankle covers, water-proof jackets, thermo lined jackets, gloves and full length tights that will adequately cover and protect your body.

In spite of the risks, there is an advantage to training in the winter no matter what the weather is. First, there are fewer riders out and the more popular cycling routes are much less crowded. Secondly, if you have the same aversion to boring gym workouts as I do, you can get some really interesting exercise and then join the gym rats in the Jacuzzi.

Heading South

When all else fails and you simply do not want to go outside in the winter, do what the pros do, go south in the winter, or for those closer to Antarctica, go north. This solution is a great one; plan a vacation in the winter and tour parts of Southern California, Florida, Mississippi, Alabama, and Arizona when it's not hot enough to fry eggs on the sidewalk. Short of buying the cycling villa in the south of Spain or in South Africa, a one or two week jaunt to warmer climes with the bike in tow can work wonders on the mid-winter blues.

Several collegiate teams plan trips for winter and spring breaks with warmer climates as the focus for early season training. Some of the favorite destinations are Florida, San Diego, and Arizona.

Retirees who follow the sun and have the ability to move south for the winter enjoy year-round warm weather cycling. A former student of mine is now the e-commerce manager of a large motor home dealership. He sells luxury motor homes on line and then offers a very convenient parts and supplies service that guarantees overnight delivery to keep the "snow-birds" on the move. When selling a motor home, in addition to inevitable questions about the furnace, television antennas, awnings, gas mileage, and the capacity of the sewage holding tank, more and more customers ask about bike racks. He is astute at business and has begun outfitting sample models on the website with various types of bicycle racks the customer can buy and have the service shop install.

When living in Boulder, I met several ambitious tri-athletes and competitive cyclists who considered the length and severity of the Boulder winters and chose to seek employment and housing in San Diego in order to train year round. The thought of getting up at seven on February the first and enjoying a seventy degree day was so much better than facing the chance of either a sixty-five degree day or a day where the temperature dipped below zero. During the brave Saturday rides where the wind could whip up to sixty miles an hour easily, the bravest Boulderites would openly chide the drop outs.

Others openly flaunt their love of the cold like the Minnesota Human Powered Vehicle Association who, in February of 2006, sponsored their annual ice race. Their web site at http://mnhpva. org/Ice/Ice2006Info.html suggests the ice over Lake Rogers is "good except for some cracking." Their rules include a ban on any kind of traction device, and all racers must have a method of stopping themselves on ice without hitting other racers. There were three races: a 100-meter time trial, a fifty-meter drag race and five-lap ice race. The web site assures the entrants they have access to the St. Thomas Academy warming hut and toilets. So much for following the sun.

It is not difficult to adapt to the cold, wet or icy weather above the mason Dixon. It is possible to maintain a very aggressive training schedule in Seattle, Buffalo, Duluth, and even Regina. Many do it every year. This plan does require careful attention to any damage to muscle and a keen sense of how to dress for the wet and cold.

APPENDIX THREE

Internet Resources

Health and Fitness Sites

www.rajeun.net/sarcopenia.html
Some interesting information on the dangers of a sedentary life as we grow older.

www.bodybuildingforyou.com/articles-submit/tom-venuto/ aerobics-muscle-loss.htm
More information on how we prevent muscle loss with proper exercise.

www.thehealthierlife.co.uk/article/3038/muscle-loss.html
The perspective e on preventing muscle loss is a bit different at this site, but also very interesting.

http://216.185.112.5/presenter.jhtml?identifier=814
The American Heart Association provides tips on how to exercise at this site. These tips are worth reading by anyone who is getting back into a fitness program.

www.agingblueprint.org/tips.cfm
This site offers several good tips on exercising, eating, safety, and fitness.

Bicycle Commuting Information

**www.sacramento-tma.org/Bicycling.htm#Characteristics%20of%
20the%20Bicycle%20Commuter**

A very good site for bicycle commuting information in Sacramento. This could serve as a model for other cities.

www.bicyclesource.com/you/commuting/employer-benefits.shtml

This site is useful for people who are considering their own personal bicycle commuting plan and for companies who want to encourage bicycle commuting.

www.crazycolour.com/os/hb04-04.shtml

This site is a bit 'off the wall,' but the tips they provide on bicycle commuting are well worth considering.

Bicycling Politics

www.bikesnotbombs.org/youth-prog.htm

This is a very good site with information on how bicycles are used to help teens learn useful skills and how to get bikes into the hands of the less fortunate.

www.bike4peace.org/

This site hosts information about the group interviewed in the book. You can follow their progress across the country on their summer ride and the progress with their activism in general.

www.commissionersam.com/node/857

This is an interesting site where Commissioner Sam Adams of Portland offers his constituents the opportunity to sound off on local issues on his site. Of particular note are the threads regarding bicycles.

www.securityworld.com/infocenter/cyclists-facing-road-rage/

This website is ordinarily devoted to issues relating to security in general, but this page focuses on how road rage is a security issue.

www.leighday.co.uk/doc.asp?doc=474&cat=845
A law firm in England hosts this site and offers information on how they have successfully sued over road rage incidents.

Interesting Bicycling Portals

Portals offer users of the internet a focused and usually well-indexed list of websites closely related to one particular topic, in this case cycling.

www.bicyclepaper.com/bp/Links/links.htm
The Bicycle Paper is a Seattle institution and their portal offers many interesting sites.

www.tenlinks.com/cycling/portals.htm
This is a link site to other link sites, all well worth the time and very informative.

www.wrenchscience.com/ws1/Support/links.asp
This site is for the ultimate tool and part fanatic. It offers information on almost any part from almost every manufacturer.

www.angelfire.com/electronic/ultramentor/links.html
This site links you to several very interesting fitness resources including associations, magazines, and other publications.

City and County Bicycle Planning Sites

www.carfree.com/link/fpor.html
This site is devoted to the concept of being "Car Free."

www.seattle.gov/transportation/bikecode.htm
Seattle's new bike plan is here.

www.denvergov.org/dephome.asp?depid=598
The Denver Bicycle plan noted in the book can be found here.

www.bicyclinginfo.org/pp/exemplary.htm
This site lists several urban/metropolitan bicycle plans. Spend some time here and compare the philosophies about bicycles in general.

www.cityofboston.gov/transportation/accessboston/bicycle.asp
The Boston bicycle plan; note in particular the "Intermodal" model.

www.sdcbc.org/
This site hosts information about the comprehensive bicycle plan in San Diego County.

Bicycle Racing Sites

www.cyclingnews.com/
An Australian site that offers in-depth racing analysis.

http://cycling.tv/
Cycling.tv has excellent live race coverage and is well worth the small fee.

www.velonews.com/
Based in Boulder, VeloNews has been one of the strongest voices in racing news for years.

www.brownielocks.com/tourdefrance.html
A history of the Tour de France.

www.umcycling.com/faq1.htm
One of the best on-line resources for track racing.

www.velogirls.com/racing/roster.php
Here they are, the Velo Girls. I listed their favorite foods in the book.

www.haulnass.com/riders_team.php
And the folks from Colorado on the Haul 'n Ass Racing Team.

Glossary

Blue line: There are two lines around a bicycle track used by racers to place themselves in strategic positions. The first line along the flat portion of the track is the blue line, and then as the bank of the track gets steeper, one encounters the red line.

BMX: Bicycle moto-cross

Camelbak: A brand of backpack featuring a water supply, accessible to the rider at any time via tubing.

Campagnolo: Italian bicycle part manufacturer.

Category (Cat) One, Cat Two, Cat Three, Cat Four and Cat Five: Categories of racing skill and success. Adults who are just beginning their racing usually begin as Cat Five and as they complete a certain number of races within a category or begin to win, they progress up to as high as Cat One, and/or sign a contract with a team and turn pro.

Criterium (crit for short): A race usually on city streets consisting of relatively short course with tight, difficult cornering.

Crank and Plank: Expression referring to sports enthusiasts who enjoy both cycling and skiing.

Cyclo-cross: Usually of road racing through grass, mud, trails and over man made and natural obstacles requiring the cyclist to dismount and carry the bike.

Drafted: This is when people ride behind someone fighting a head wind; the cyclist in front acts as a shield for the rider behind, making life much more pleasant. In fact, people who always draft behind other riders often forget there is such a thing as a head wind.

Dropped (to be): Cyclists run in packs to reduce wind resistance. If you can't keep up with the pack, you are dropped. A pack can be huge, hundreds of riders, or rather small.. You can also just be dropped from a big group. This often happens in the mountains.

Drop out: A slot in the frame or fork of a bicycle where the axle of the wheel is attached.

Gearing the cassette: The cassette is the cluster of gears at the back of the bike. Gearing the cassette means selecting the cassette to have the correct gears: a flat run would have tiny gears, a mountain run would have bigger gears.

Ochsner: A brand of bicycle built in Switzerland; the company is better known there for making garbage trucks but the bikes are really good.

Omnium: A two- or three-day race, usually seen in collegiate racing, that includes a team time trial, a criterium and a road race. Points are earned for placing within the top twenty spots and the winner has the highest total points from the three events.

Sarcopenia: The degenerative loss of skeletal muscle mass and strength in senescence. About a third of muscle mass is lost. This loss of mass reduces the performance of muscles.

Scratch race: A track race where all cyclists start on the same scratch (line) on the track, usually for a designated distance or number of laps.

Time Trials: Whether individual or team, this is a race pitting one person or one team against another. Individuals or teams ride alone over the same course and the winner is simply the fastest.

Tensiometer: A tool that measures the tension in a spoke allowing mechanics to achieve precise tensions on all spokes.

Torelli: A brand of bicycle made in Italy.

Track Bike: A bike with a fixed rear gear and no shifting levers or brakes. The rider has only positive motion; that is when the wheels move so do the pedals. Urban legend suggests cyclist are regularly thrown off track bikes because of this, but this is not true. Most good cyclists know how to use their leg motion for braking.

Truing Wheels: The art and science of properly adjusting spokes so the wheel rolls straight.

U23: Age group indicating the racers are all under 23 years of age.

Velodrome: A track designated for bicycle track racing.

Yellow Jersey: In French, the *maillot jaune,* is the jersey worn by the current overall leader of the Tour de France, allowing the rider who was in the overall lead at the end of the previous day to be easily identified during the race.

Index

About the Author

Photo courtesy of Mary Stoural.

Shawn Rohrbach was born in Seattle on April 16, 1956. He was raised (although he has not quite yet grown up) in the mountains of the Cascade Range at the summit of Snoqualmie Pass. He graduated from Mt Si High School in Snoqualmie, Washington, and completed his bachelor of arts degree at the Seminary of Christ the King, operated by the Benedictine Monks of Westminster Abbey in Mission, British Columbia.

He completed his master of fine arts at the Jack Kerouac School of Disembodied Poetics, known now as Naropa University in Boulder, Colorado. He earned his certificate in the Fundamentals of Bicycle Mechanics and the Advanced Certificate in Wheel Building from the Bend Bicycle Workshop in Bend Oregon under the guidance of Joe Bianculli. Currently Shawn serves as the Associate Dean of Technology at ITT Technical Institute in Everett, Washington.

Contests, new titles, events, news, discussion and feedback. Sign up for your latest chance to win, and find out about upcoming books at **www.dreamtimepublishing.com**

OUR COMMUNITY

DreamTime Publishing supports the community by participating regularly in worthwhile fundraising and charitable efforts. Let us know what's important to you, and sign up at **www.dreamtimepublishing.com** to find out what's happening near you.

ONLINE BOOK CLUB AND MORE!

Come by and share in a discussion of the latest books from top authors and leave your feedback on DreamTime Publishing's titles and for our authors. Sign up at **www.dreamtimepublishing.com** to get the latest information.

WHAT'S GOING ON?

Check out our online calendar for events and appearances by DreamTime authors. Sign up at **www.dreamtimepublishing.com** to make sure you don't miss anything!